Jonathan Holroyd

Accountancy
It's Your Business

97 ideas to help your accountancy practice
become a great accountancy business

First published 2017 by
Added Value Solutions,
7 Midland Way,
Derbyshire S43 4XA

This edition published 2017
A catalogue for this book is available in the British Library

Edited by Nancy Callegari
Typeset by Charles Bradshaw
Printed and bound in the UK

ISBN 978-0-9957562-0-5

Contents

Preface

If you are reading this, it is probably because you are either a prospect, new or existing member of AVN. If you are an existing member then you will know exactly what this outstanding organisation can do for you, your accountancy business and your clients (or customers as I like to call them). If you are a prospect or new member, you are likely to be unsure and uncertain of what your future membership holds for you.

Let me tell you. If you embrace all the things AVN suggests to you and take the appropriate action, it will transform you, your business and also your clients. It will, because it did just that for me and the accountancy business of Hunter Gee Holroyd (HGH).

In the introduction of this book you will learn how it was the catalyst for enormous change for both myself and the business. Was it an overnight success? Did everything work first time? Did we get immediate payback? No, of course it wasn't and we didn't! It took a long time and is still ongoing today. You will read what Mark Grewer (he acquired my share in the business) has to say about HGH today and how the process continues.

Put simply though, you have to take action! Do some of the stuff which AVN suggests and when it seems as though you are going uphill or wading through treacle, just keep on doing it! Those who persist will gain the rewards. Those who give up, well... I am not sure what they get. Perhaps more of the same old stuff they got before. And that is not what you want, otherwise why become a prospective or new member? You do so because you want something different. So, go on. **Do it!**

Jonathan Holroyd

Foreword
by Steve Pipe

This is an astonishingly useful and practical book for any accountant who wants to make their practice more successful. Having known the author for almost 20 years, this comes as no surprise to me.

Jonathan has spent his life working with accountants, initially building and leading an award-winning multi-office practice in Yorkshire (where they call a spade a spade), and then visiting, advising and coaching hundreds of accountants across the UK (where he also always "says it as it is").

And, as you will see as you read these pages, his experience, passion and insights are second to none.

If you are an AVN member you will instantly see where his words of wisdom are coming from. You will find them invaluable in accelerating your success with all things AVN and you will really appreciate the appendices pointing you to the most relevant and useful supporting AVN tools and resources.

If you aren't an AVN member you will probably find Jonathan's words of wisdom even more valuable. Partly because you probably won't have read anything as useful before. And partly because they are a brilliant way to start tackling the key challenges facing most firms, a brilliant way to start making your practice more successful and profitable, and a brilliant way to start making your life more balanced, rewarding and enjoyable.

So, wherever you are in your professional life today, you are going to love this book.

And to help make sure that you do, here are my top tips for getting the most out of it:

1. How you read it us up to you: dip in and out in any order you like, or read it cover to cover. But either way, make sure you read it all. There are so many powerful insights littered across the pages, and you really can't afford to miss any of them.
2. Treat it as a work book rather than a library book – use a highlighter pen to identify the bits which resonate most with you, and annotate your thoughts in the margins.
3. Draw up a list of key insights and potential actions as you go along.
4. Share the book with everyone in your practice.
5. Arrange a meeting with your entire team to discuss their reaction to the book – and the implications for your firm.
6. Draw up an action plan – with complete clarity over who is responsible for each action, and the date by which it must be done.
7. Make your action plan easier and more profitable to implement by ensuring it makes full use of the supporting shortcuts, tools and resources listed on these pages.
8. Give someone the job of holding you accountable to make sure the things on your action plan are actually completed.

By doing these eight things you will make life better for you and your family, your team and their families, along with your clients and their families.

So, what are you waiting for?

How AVN Can Help
A message from Shane Lukas,
Managing Director of AVN

Now, more than ever before, accountants need to do far more for their clients than merely providing compliance accounts and basic business services such as payroll, bookkeeping and management information. This is essential for your practice to survive and for you to be of any meaningful service to your clients going forward.

Technology evolves more in just one single hour than it has in the previous 100 years, and that includes the previous hour!

As technology evolves so does the software we all use and the intelligence behind the software. Artificial intelligence is predicted to match that of the human brain by 2023, based on current exponential growth trends.

More and more software companies are forming, which transforms the way people do business. With increasing paperless transactions and accounting technologies progressing towards 1-click solutions, traditional accountants will soon be rendered obsolete. You may not be experiencing this right now, but within the next three to five years the need for an accountant to produce compliance accounts will be redundant.

At present compliance accounts are a necessity, but because the process time is reducing so much, an accountant working in their bedroom can process these just as effectively as a large firm. This bedroom-based accountant could be situated in any country in the world; many are trained in British Accountancy legislation and provide this service online.

It's not the same as in person, but how many of your clients are you seeing regularly and having meaningful discussions with? What are you doing right now that's sufficiently different from the competition?

Are you simply allowing a client to drop off their books and records and you're dealing with these? Digital books and records and even paper based receipts can be submitted to anyone anywhere. Overseas accountants are registering UK office addresses at scanning facilities where posted paperwork is simply fed through an industrial scanner and sent across the world, received and analysed by software and largely processed before a human being even looks at them.

UK accountants can't compete with the rock bottom price these overseas accountants can charge because their cost of living is a fraction of ours.

Most business owners see compliance accounts as a necessary evil they need to have for legal reasons. Having their compliance accounts produced at rock bottom fees is appealing because they don't see the value in them.

By implementing the changes in this book, by applying the principles to your own practice and then helping the businesses you work with to apply these principles themselves you'll become more valuable. You can become a trusted advisor to your clients.

Please, don't simply give this book a read and store it on the bookshelf for years to come by way of decoration. Take the principles seriously and implement them.

If you're an AVN member we'll be taking you on a seven stage, road mapped journey that's tailored to take you from where you are right now in your practice to becoming the sought after business growth advisor to your clients, implementing business improvements strategies on your own practice along the way. This journey includes intensive help, support, training and guidance and we'll be holding you accountable to your actions.

This is a great book written by a former partner of an AVN member firm. The principles in this book have become incredibly important to Jonathan because he's seen the impact they've had on his practice and his explanations as to why they're important are based on his experience and the results he's seen.

For AVN members, as you have access to a plethora of great resources at your fingertips, I've included an additional paragraph at the end of many of the points of advice that Jonathan's given, highlighting how AVN helps you make this stuff happen far more effectively than going it alone. I've mentioned above our seven stage AVN roadmap journey. Almost everything listed in this book is covered as part of these roadmaps and so I will refrain from referring to them as much as possible, Instead, I will highlight additional resources available for you to pull up immediately.

Occasionally I make reference to a tool called GoalGetter, a tool jointly created by AVN and Jonathan himself. It's a great tool to use to drill down into key areas of a business to ascertain both a current situation analysis and to determine goals. It also produces a template business plan which can be developed. This can be applied to your practice and as a tool to work with clients on their business. As this is a joint product it is subject to a separate arrangement. For more information about GoalGetter talk to our team at AVN.

If you're not an AVN member and would like additional information and get access to resources to help you implement some of this learning and more, go to www.improveyourpractice.co.uk

This is a wonderful book, kindly gifted to AVN to distribute at its discretion to accountants throughout the country to help them recognise the potential their practice can have on its owner(s), its team and its clients.

> *Shane Lukas, Author of The Business Owner's Guide to the UK's Best Accountancy Practices and What's Next for Accountants – How to overcome the biggest threat yet facing the profession.*

Introduction

I had been a Chartered Accountant for around 40 years, nine of which were as a sole practitioner and 21 years in a partnership. For the next ten years or so I was helping other accountants run a better business of their own. What gives me the qualifications to do that? Well, you may read this book and say "clearly not a lot." However, I think I have because, I learnt late in life that you need to change and stop being just an accountant who acts as a professional accountant, but become an accountant who runs an accountancy business.

When I was in my fiftieth year, (I was born in 1947) I was so tired of the business I was in that I wanted to get out as soon as I could. I had a mid- life crisis. I remember seeing the very attractive practice nurse for my fifty-year service check up, and I am embarrassed to say that I broke down and cried. Thankfully she listened and told me that I needed to change things in my life. I recall walking down the street afterwards and thinking 'I can do anything I like. I don't have to continue doing what I'm currently doing.' I have since told her how much I owe her.

As a result of that Eureka moment, my wife and I bought a newsagency business in Easingwold, where we lived. It was the typical run down CTN business, confectionary, tobacco and newspapers shop. I negotiated my retirement over a five-year period and cut back to a four day week at the office and started working three days a week in the newsagents. Getting up at 5am to go and sort out the papers was infinitely more fun than going to work as an accountant. That shows how sad I had become. We worked very hard at building the business up and we eventually sold it three years later with doubled turnover. I learnt an enormous amount from that little business. It made me realise how some of my clients felt. I knew more of their issues and I felt I could help them. They found it fascinating to know that I had another life outside of accountancy and could talk 'their language'. I understood more about 'footfall', 'average spends', 'up-sales' and all the other stuff that goes with it.

After I realised I could help my newsagency clients, and I had a
few, it dawned on me that my 'retailing clients' could benefit
from my experiences. One retailing business is much like the
next as similar issues apply to them all. It occurred to me that as
many businesses have common issues, I really could help all
businesses. This got me really quite excited. I felt reborn.
Suddenly the accountancy business seemed more exciting.

Many of you will have heard of Paul Dunn and the 'boot-camp'.
In October 1998 we had the opportunity to go to one of his
'awareness days', and this was quite an experience. Despite
myself and fellow partner seeing that it could benefit our
practice, we did worry about its 'evangelical' side and so we did
nothing. Then about six weeks later I went to see Steve Pipe in
Leeds. Steve did something similar and he called it the Added
Value Network. The message was very much the same, but it
was in 'English' and I felt my partners would accept it more
readily. Two of us (Mark Grewer and myself – you will read what
Mark has to say a little later) went on the AVN MasterClass in
May 1999.

It was the catalyst for enormous change in my life and the
business life of Hunter Gee Holroyd.

Through the AVN I met Graham Lamont of Lamont Pridmore in
Workington. Graham worked with HGH for about nine months
and we learnt even more! Previously we had not been a very
efficient business. We lacked leadership and profits. We were a
typical 'professional accountancy practice', going nowhere fast.
In fact, we were probably going backwards. Graham made us see
that we needed to become an accountancy business and start to
run our business in the same way as we would advise our clients
to run theirs.

In 1997 one of our very many initiatives, and thankfully one
which was successful, was to start providing financial services
to our clients and we formed a limited company to do just that.
As a Director in this company my name must have found its way
onto a mailing list and I received a 'flyer' from the Institute of

Directors in conjunction with Durham Business School about the Institute of Directors' 'Certificate in Company Direction'. This was a course of 15 days spread over six months, covering ten modules. When I read the syllabus, I realised that I needed to complete it. It complemented perfectly everything I was learning through membership of the AVN and also the experiences of working with Graham. It was expensive, but worth every single penny. You see, I was becoming a bit of a learning junky! Reading the books that Steve Pipe recommended had fired my enthusiasm further and really was opening my mind to all sorts of ideas and opportunities.

From May 1999 through to December 2002, when I retired, HGH changed. We changed the culture in the business. We changed from being a professional accountancy practice to a business which happened to be in the business of accountancy. We built and created a fantastic team of people. They told us that they had great leaders and we were more profitable. Was everything perfect? No, of course it wasn't. There was still a lot to do, as there always will be, but we had made a fantastic start.

Steve Pipe asked me what I was going to do in my retirement and to be truthful I was not sure at that time. He asked me if I would like to work with AVN as he thought other firms might benefit from some of my experiences. Since January 2003, I have made over 350 visits to accountancy businesses, varying from sole practitioners with very low fees to multi-partner practices with quite substantial fees. Like HGH, they all had issues which needed addressing. Are they always the same? No, they are not, but very often they are or they are a mix of the same. You see, the biggest problem we as accountants have, is that we are not trained to be business owners! We are trained to be accountants. How does an accountant usually become a partner in a multi-partner practice? Usually by being technically very good at what he/she does. Nobody becomes a partner because they have great business skills and perhaps that needs to change. We all need to develop our business skills. So, start thinking of your practice as a business. Start to think of your clients as customers.

I hope that in the following pages some of the ideas referred to will help you become a better business owner. No single thing makes a business great. It's thousands of little things all working in harmony which will do that. If you put the ideas in this book into place I am certain that your accountancy business will improve, and as a result you will be a more successful, happier person who has successful and happy clients.

This book is not an academic book and it was never intended to be. It started out as a way of simply capturing some of the things I have learnt from a number of people, mostly over the last 20 years or so. The order of the ideas is a bit haphazard, mainly because it was a bit of a brain dump. One thing leads to another and there is a thread through most of it.

Most of what I have written is common sense. Nothing clever at all! The only clever bit is that common sense is not commonly used. So, if you practice using common sense, perhaps you will be cleverer than many others.

I hope that some of the ideas make you think. I hope that most will be helpful to you, but remember they only work if you take action to make them work. This is the biggest mistake many of us make. We think about something but we do nothing.

Be brave, take action and make things happen!

How AVN Helped Develop
Our Business Services

Hello, I am Mark Grewer. I am the guy Jonathan referred to in his introduction and the one who attended the AVN MasterClass with him in 1999. I qualified in 1995 after being a student with HGH. I then had two years post-qualification experience with them. In this period I saw Jonathan become increasingly frustrated with life at work, although at the time I was not sure why.

I have never really liked auditing and did not want to pursue a career in this field so in 1997, when Jonathan asked me if I was interested in buying his share in the practice I virtually snapped his hand off. I had a chance to actually run an accountancy business. Subsequent to this, in May 1999 we attended the AVN MasterClass and it opened my eyes to all sorts of new possibilities.

We were, at that time, a very ordinary firm offering professional compliance services. However, because of our AVN membership we started offering new services and most importantly we started helping our clients to improve their businesses. This was not an overnight process and in a long established practice like ours it can and did take a long time. The process continues to this day. In simple terms, our previous offering was – "Here are your accounts, this is what you will have to pay in tax and this is our bill!"

In addition to the basic services, we now offer business planning, forecasting and budgeting, inheritance tax planning, exit planning and strategies, ideas and strategies for profit growth, improvements in customer service and many others. Initially using AVN content, in 2006 we also set up monthly seminars for clients and contacts. We are still running them today. It is not technical content, but it is about ways of improving your business and your life!

As a result, we are not the same accountancy practice we were in 1999. We are more of an accountancy business. With fixed fees and clients paying in advance and by Direct Debit, our debtor days and WIP lock up are a third of what they were previously. We have, as a business, grown immensely and now look after a range of great quality clients who genuinely want us to help them with not only the basic compliance stuff, but also help them in their businesses, and as a result improve the quality of their lives.

We have also changed the culture in the business, ceasing to be 'us as bosses' and 'them as employees'. We are now a team of 37 people who are all actively involved in the business and everyone is entrusted to provide a great service. This is what we all endeavour to do.

Mark Grewer, Head of HGH Corporate Finance

List Of Ideas

01 Have Congruent Goals

Many accountancy businesses have multiple business owners. Very often these owners do not understand their own goals, let alone the goals of their co-business owners. Then they wonder why things don't appear to be moving in the right direction. The most successful businesses have congruent goals.

This means the business owners have personal goals which are understood by one another and these personal goals are congruent to the overall business goals (the vision). I have worked with business owners and got them to think about and then articulate their personal goals. In doing so, and making them listen to one another, it has become apparent to them that they are simply not compatible with one another. How can the business achieve anything when they all seem to want different things from it? It cannot! So, the only wise thing to do is to realise things need to change and that probably means having different owners or having more than one business. They get a divorce. Painful I know, but far less painful than continuing to struggle, as they surely would, if they continue to strive for different things. However, in many cases the business owners do want many things to be compatible. They just do not know what each wants and more importantly, they do not make sure that business goals are aligned to personal goals.

Does this apply if you are a sole practitioner? Yes, it does, as you must make sure that your business goals reflect what it is you want in your personal life. They must be congruent! Have a vision for your business that gives you what you want personally. If you don't, you don't have a business, you have a job! Working for yourself that's all!

So, set about defining your personal goals and share them with your partners, if you have any. You may find this exercise difficult. You may find it easy. However, experience shows that it may be worth your while thinking about having a facilitator to assist in the process. An outsider who is skilled in asking probing questions and good at listening to the answers! Just the sort of skills that you need to acquire if you don't already have them. This person can then help with the sharing process, keep everybody on track and ensure that you don't wander off and that you ultimately address what may be difficult issues.

HOW AVN CAN HELP
This is a crucial first step with AVN. As part of your induction we take you through a process of ascertaining specific goals as part of the AVN Roadmap. There's a resource in System Builder called the 24-hour goal setting tool you can work through which helps you ascertain what the most important numbers are to you and then helps you set goals around making those numbers better. Simply type 'goal setting' into the search tool in System Builder.
GoalGetter will assist you in clarifying congruent personal and business goals.

02 Have A Vision

Yep, you've heard it many times before and you've probably thought – 'Yes, I'll have one of those', and then thought, 'Umm, how do I get one?' And then, after you've struggled to get one, thought 'Why do I need one anyway?' It was Stephen Covey in his much read and respected book 'The 7 Habits of Highly Effective People' who said (second habit), "Start with the end in mind." If you don't know what you want, how are you going to know how to start to achieve it? How will you know when you've got it? All successful people know what it is they want and they do this by picturing the final outcome. What's it going to look like when I have built this business?

Remember, I said that your personal goals need to be congruent with your business goals. What you want for your business must give you what you want in your personal life. If you make a list of your business goals, making sure they do not conflict with your personal goals, you are starting to frame up your vision – your picture of your business. A business vision is only a list of business goals strung together with some words, but it is ultimately the picture of your business when it is finished. A business that will give you what you want for both yourself and those important in your life.

However, some people find it difficult to paint and draw, so imagining what your business is going to look like is not easy for us all. I have found that the best way to start to picture something is by putting numbers in the picture. Yes, I know it sounds like I am talking about painting with numbers, but in a way I am. Most business owners will know the turnover they want to achieve and when they want to achieve it. Most want a level of profitability in that timescale, so it naturally follows that you can put a number on that. Whoops, if I need that profitability, then I am going to have to increase my turnover. If I need that turnover how many people must I employ and do I have big enough premises? That starts to get you understanding what your wage/salary costs are and what your overheads will be. Anyway, I thought you wanted to build a great business and that means you may need to pay a percentage above the average salary costs in my business sector and our customers services. Instead of measuring a measly four out of ten, it needs to be at least an eight out of ten to get us that turnover.

Great businesses don't rely upon the business owners because they have systems which allow others to do the work just as brilliantly as you do. This means that you can take eight to ten weeks' holiday a year and only work a 40-hour week! Now I know it varies from one accountancy business to another, but I bet you can now start to think about the type of clients you will want and how many you will need and how much the average fee is going to be to give you that turnover. If you need that many clients how many potential clients will you need and what is your conversion rate going to have to be? How many times will they buy from you?

You see its all numbers! Numbers start the picture off. Once you get the numbers sorted and they all work together, you are on the way to starting to build a vision of your business. The great thing about numbers is – they don't lie! Well, they do if you want them to – but a 10 is a 10 in anybody's language and so is £1,000,000. You get what I mean? It's a great starting point and a lot better than telling everybody 'My business is going to be the best in the world'. Great statement, but what does it really mean? If you want to explain to any third person just what your business is going to be, can you tell them these things?

- In the accounting period ended 30th June 20**.
- By that time there will be * directors/partners in the business.
- Our customers' services measured on a scale of 1–10 by our customers will have been an average of * in that year (striving for a 10).
- Its turnover will be £*.
- Its net profit before tax will be £*.
- It will employ * people.
- They will be remunerated at *% above the average in this business sector.
- We will operate from * square feet.
- We will have * number of clients.
- They will buy on average * times a year with an average spend of £*.
- I will be working a * hour week and taking * weeks holiday a year.

And so on and so on...

All these things and more will paint a clear picture of what your business is and what it will look like when it's finished.

To help you create your vision use the following 'grid' to help you think about all the key issues, where you are now and where you want to be. There may be many other aspects that you wish to add. This is only the start. And remember, what you want for your business, MUST give you what you want for you personally.

KEY ISSUES	NOW	IN _____ YEARS FROM NOW
Number of business owners		
Turnover/Revenue		
Net profit before tax		
Borrowings		
Size of team (no. of people)		
Geographic location		
How many offices?		
Size of your premises		
Type of products and services		
Number of customers		
Ideal customer		
Market share		
Customer delight		
Team happiness		

HOW AVN CAN HELP

As with goals, developing your vision is covered at the same time as part of your induction with AVN – your Practice Growth Expert will help you with your vision and for additional help in this area simply type 'vision' into System Builder for a wealth of additional online learning and help. These include two online training courses entitled 'Goals, Mission, Vision and Strategy' – a presentation by Steve Pipe, and 'Your Vision, Your Numbers' – a presentation by Jonathan Holroyd (as a guest speaker at an AVN event).

GoalGetter is designed to leave no stone unturned as it prompts thought in every aspect of business and helps the business owner ascertain exactly what they aspire toward in each of those areas.

03 Understand Your Mission

Many people have heard they should have a business mission. Well, that's got you excited, hasn't it? Yep, the best thing to come out of America was the need to have a business mission statement. They were all the rage in the late eighties and early nineties. We all had them plastered over our walls and told our 'staff' they should 'sign up' to them and then went off to run our businesses in exactly the same way as we always had.

The trouble is that not many people really understand what a mission statement really is. If you and your team understand and work to your mission, you may achieve business success. It's all about understanding why you are in business. Exactly that! What are you here for? What is your purpose? What difference is your business going to make to the lives of your customers? Richard Dobbins and Barrie O Pettman in the book 'The Ultimate Entrepreneurs Book' say that the mission of every business should be "to enrich the lives of its customers." How is your business going to do that?

Mission statements do not need to be long. In fact, preferably they should be short, so that everyone understands and believes in them. They can sometimes be a 'strap line' in your marketing. Something that is memorable, but believable. A mission statement should be powerful and inspirational. Something special that will get you noticed. However, a word of caution! If you don't believe in it, don't have it. They are not things to be cynically displayed, because 'we need to have one'.

The following questions, if discussed and fully understood, will help you understand and ultimately help you define your business mission.

1. What are we really selling?
2. What are our customers really buying from us? (Note – this answer is likely to be different to the one asked in question 1)
3. How are we being really different from other accountants?
4. What is our U S P (unique selling proposition)?
5. Why did we go into business?
6. How are we going to change people's lives?
7. How will people remember our business?
8. How are we going to make a difference?

HOW AVN CAN HELP

Type 'mission' into the System Builder knowledge base search box and open the Action Resource entitled 'How to create the perfect mission statement.'

Also, understanding your mission/purpose forms part of the AVN Roadmap journey and is covered specifically during a workshop day.

GoalGetter will also take you through thought provoking questions that will help you ascertain your mission.

04 Understand Where Your Business Is Now

Many business owners do not understand where their business is NOW. It's vitally important to understand this. I can hear you say "but what if I am only starting a business, what does it matter and anyway, what do you mean by understanding where I am now?"

Have you ever heard of the 'Sigmoid Curve?' Charles Handy refers to it in his book 'The Empty Raincoat.'

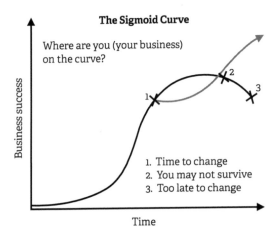

The Sigmoid Curve

Where are you (your business) on the curve?

Business success

1. Time to change
2. You may not survive
3. Too late to change

Time

It's all about the simple theory that nothing lasts forever. Everything changes and it does not matter whether it's one hour, or a millennium, nothing stays the same.

So, for example what you sell today will only have a certain lifespan. How many businesses which started a hundred years ago are still around today? Very few. We all know the pace of change is frightening and it's not going to slow down. Knowing where you are now in your business life cycle is critical to your survival. Where are you on the curve? If you are at the top it's already too late to bring about change. If you are over the top you may not survive. To be effective you need to take action before you get to the top, and start another curve (upwards of course). You may find things do not improve straight away, but they will improve and get even better. You can see that the 'Sigmoid Curve' principle applies to everything about your business, your products or services and your markets etc. That's why you need to constantly ask yourself the question, "Where am I now?"

There are lots of diagnostic tools to help you with this process. The best and oldest is probably the SWOT analysis. The Strengths, Weaknesses, Opportunities and Threats analysis is a great process to enable you to clearly understand the issues in your business and we will talk about this a little more, later on in the book. There are others such as PEEST analysis (Political, Environmental, Economical, Social and Technological) and PORTERS FIVE FORCES, but in their way they are only, in my opinion, more sophisticated SWOT's. Perhaps there is an argument though, to use them if your business has large markets, many products/services and much competition.

SWOT's, and how best to carry them out in order to get some fantastic information about your business, are referred to later in this book.

HOW AVN CAN HELP
GoalGetter will help with situation analysis. Type 'swot' in to System Builder to get access to the template. The template contains incredibly helpful, thought provoking questions against each section which will help when conducting the exercise.

05 Have A Passion For What You Do

If you have a hobby, it's usually because you enjoy doing it! You have heard people say that their job is their hobby. I bet you've thought 'I wish I felt that about my job'. Well, if you don't like doing what you are doing, why are you doing it? If it's just to pay the mortgage, it's not a business but another job. You are just working for yourself that's all.

Have you ever experienced it when someone has told you about their business, perhaps when they are about to set/start it up? They are full of excitement and enthusiasm. They are infectious and you really want it to succeed. That's how you should be about your business! If you aren't excited, how do you expect anyone else to be? How are you going to motivate your employees if you do not really believe in your business and its 'mission?' You need to show passion for what you do. If you don't get excited about this business. go and run another one; a business where you can get excited! Passion is vital if you are to enthuse and excite those you employ. If you want them to be motivated, you need to be motivated.

> **HOW AVN CAN HELP**
> This is an exercise we take you through during a workshop event which forms part of AVN Roadmap 2. There is a great video available on YouTube by Simon Sinek on this very subject that's highly worth watching. Simply type these four keywords into YouTube and it will appear first in the listing: tedx simon sinek 2009
> His book 'Start with Why', Simon Sinkek, is excellent too.

06 Have A Business Plan

All businesses need a business plan and your accountancy business is no different. Not a dusty old binder with a hundred sheets of paper which stays on the shelf, but a living, moving, measuring plan which gets referred to consistently and gets used in many ways. There is nothing complicated about a business plan. If there is, it's probably not a good one. A business plan is a list of actions glued together with words, that's all. Once you have set your 'vision' and you understand your 'mission' i.e. your purpose and you know 'where you are now', what you have strategies to get you there. That's why total clarity about these three things. If Glasgow and you are planning your route, where you are starting. If you think you are find you are actually in Bristol, you are going to confused as to the route and will either end up w time and petrol or you may never get there at all be has broken down. A business plan is your sat nav.

The strategies are the route you will take. Sometimes those strategies will change and that's why you need to consistently ask yourself the right questions. When you are on a route, you usually measure the miles! The same applies in your business. You need to measure the progress you are making. That's where the 'one page business plan' comes into it. We will talk about that later. Anyway, the expression 'what you can measure, you can manage' is true and measuring your progress enables you to determine the next steps and helps you decide, 'Am I on the right track? Do I need to change anything?'

What should a business plan contain? It may depend upon the reason the plan was prepared. However, in general the plan should (I contend) contain the following:

1. A summary of the business vision, using numbers as they are measurable and more meaningful.
2. A short statement as to the business mission (What's your purpose and what difference are you going to make? How are you going to change your customers' lives?)
3. A summary of your current position. Where are you now in relation to your market place, products/services, customers etc?
4. What are your marketing strategies going to be? What are your new products/services? Who are your new customers? What is your pricing policy? What image/brand will you have, etc?
5. What about your people? How are you going to recruit, reward, appraise, train, and involve your people?

t business has systems
as you can do them

ou going to need?
f all of this? What

The actions you
the action, who
pecific!

t to put it in
eresting and
f and who
perhaps, but then
to keep the content relevant
it gets used.

you need to review it? I would suggest at least once a year and more often in some businesses. And if you are measuring your progress it is getting reviewed on an ongoing basis anyway. At least once a month.

HOW AVN CAN HELP

Our AVN Excellence model driven forward through the AVN Roadmaps helps you define a Business Plan. For additional help go into the System Builder Knowledge Base to find a training resource on 'Business Planning,' and as mentioned previously type in 'Goals, Mission, Vision and Strategy.' In addition, GoalGetter can help with this process.

07 Benchmark Your Business – Regularly

A great way to understand part of 'where we are now' is to benchmark your business against others in your sector. It's also a great way to measure your progress, although it can be a bit scary and mind blowing to do it. Perhaps you might not be a good as you thought you were, but that's a good thing, isn't it? Finding out, I mean! Now you know some of the challenges you face it will either inspire you or make you want to give up or even do something else. Benchmarking your business will give you some focus and highlight the areas where the greatest improvement is required. Any one of those results is better than just 'battling on' hoping that some day everything will come good.

HOW AVN CAN HELP

AVN provides AVNBenchMark, a tool that accountants across the UK have been using to benchmark their own practice and to benchmark their clients for many years. This means a well-established, extensive database of comparable data exists.

As mentioned, BenchMark can be used to benchmark your own practice as well as your clients. There are additional accountancy practice specific data fields available when benchmarking an accountancy practice which provides further details, analysis and comparison. This tool also produces highly impactful reports.

AVN members benchmark their own practice annually and use the tool to benchmark every single client, using the reports to aid in delivering more meaningful meetings with clients, which adds more value and often leads to additional work for the accountant.

Typing 'Benchmark' into System Builder will give you access to our BenchMark toolkit too. AVNBenchMark is available independently of AVN membership. For further information, visit **www.improveyourpractice.co.uk**

08 Involve Your Team In The Development Of Your Business

A business plan is great, but no good if nobody knows about it! The best business plans are developed by the people who work in the business. That means everybody, not just the business owners. How do you feel about that? Is that a bit scary too? Do you want to tell people "This is how it's going to be?" Or are you going to ask them "How do you want it to be?" The last one gets better results. I don't mean by abrogating your responsibilities, but by involving your people in the process of developing your plan. This is where certain skills in people management are important. We will talk about that later, but getting the balance right here is critical. I know some people who just like to be told what's happening. I know some people who just want to be led, but they like to be asked for an opinion! I know some people who like to be consulted about everything, but they like others to take the decisions. Do you know your people? What do they like?

I also know that if you want people to carry out a task, it's more likely that task will get done if the person doing it understands why it's being done, and better still if the person suggested it be done in the first place. Is this making any kind of sense?

Your business plan will have lots of actions. You want to make sure they get done. After all, nothing happens unless you take action. If your employees are involved in the development of the plan and suggest some of the actions, there is a greater likelihood of them happening and with the right results. This section is not about 'how to manage people', but if you can manage people effectively you will have more success. Getting their input into the plan is critical to its overall success. Involve them at the outset. Ask them questions like, 'What do you think to the vision for the business?' 'Is it ambitious?' 'Do you understand what we are trying to achieve?' 'What do you think?' 'How do you think we can achieve this?'

Perhaps you can ask them the questions about 'your business mission'. Have a conversation around these questions and get their input. Remember to listen closely to what they say. Use their comments in your plan or at least explain why you may not be able to. One of the biggest frustrations people have is when they do not understand why their ideas do not get used.

If you explain, you will get people's 'buy in'. If they buy into it, things get done and that's what you want, don't you?

Once you've consulted and shared the plan some finalisation of it is required, but remember, the best plans are never finished but always being improved and altered. However, more importantly than that, they are constantly referred to with progress measured against the original targets. In other words, you are keeping score.

HOW AVN CAN HELP
Team building and engagement are something that AVN are incredibly passionate about. Simply type 'team' into the System Builder Knowledge Base and you will find dozens of resources to help you to really get team involvement and buy-in.

09 Learn How To Manage People

Managing people is a skill! Some say it's all about a carrot and stick and using them in the right place and at the right time. Are some people automatically good at managing people? Maybe, but most of us need to learn how to do this more effectively. Accountants are notoriously bad at managing people and that is no real surprise. Who trained them? Nobody! Accountants trained to be accountants and that's what most of them are good at. Being an accountant!

One of the best things that ever happened to me was when I was in practice and we decided to go for Investors in People (IIP). We failed miserably at the first attempt and the main criticism was that we were bad at managing our people. It was suggested that we had some people management skills training. We had a five weekly three-hour intensive training programme, part of which was role play. I squirmed! I found myself becoming more and more embarrassed in each scenario. I could see myself reacting in a particular way, and it was not the 'right' way. I could also see how I should have reacted but failed. I had to change and it was difficult. I had to constantly remind myself that I needed to change my behaviour. After a while I became less self-conscious and began to do it automatically. I am a lot better now than I was. Not perfect but a lot better.

One of the worst things was the change in my moods. I was never the same person from one day to the next. It was pointed out on more than one occasion that my mood when I came into the office on a morning determined the mood my team went home in that night. My people never knew where they were with me.

Let me give you an example. Perhaps you may even see yourself doing this.

It is a lovely summer day. You are going on holiday in three days having just arranged a last-minute deal. Your tickets for your holiday have arrived in the post. You are on top of your workload and you have a meeting with a prospect client. You meet them and they like you. They agree to your fee quote and sign up there and then. You drive back to your office and find a parking space. The sun is shining and all is well with the world. You go through the reception, fly past Julie and say "Hi Julie. Great day, isn't it?" She thinks – 'He's in a great mood. I will ask him about that pay rise I was after'. In other words, you are in a great mood and people notice it. However, do you remember the occasion when – you are back from holiday! It was good but it is over. It is your first day back and there is a mountain of work. One of your biggest and best clients has asked for an urgent meeting this afternoon. You leave the office. You see the client and he is unhappy about the fee. Despite your best efforts, they want to leave you and try this other firm who have been courting them for ages. You travel back to your office only to find someone has taken your parking space. It's raining, you have no umbrella or raincoat and you eventually get back to the office wet through. You kick open the door and march straight past Julie because you are fed up. What does Julie think of you now? Not much!

And worse still, she is confused because one day you are up and the next day you are down. You are never consistent.

I have since heard someone say that "a business owner is not allowed to have moods, only the employees are!" Perhaps that's right. You cannot stop people from bringing their home lives into their work place. That would be an unnatural thing to expect, but I guess business owners need to leave theirs at the door. A thing to remember as a business owner is, 'people do have a life out of the workplace and we should be interested in it'. As I say somewhere else in this book, "if you want to be interesting, you should be interested."

The biggest tip I would give you is to learn to be critical of yourself and the way you manage people and situations. It is difficult. Believe me it's difficult, but those who do, will be rewarded. They will constantly learn from the process.

HOW AVN CAN HELP
We provide workshop training which covers many ways of getting the best out of people and specifically focuses on understanding how very different people are. We always assume that we should treat others how we expect to be treated ourselves. In fact, that's not the case, which is why people don't always get the best out of their team. Talk to your Practice Growth Expert at AVN to find out more about our training workshops on teams.
In addition, there are great systems in System Builder you can implement right away under the section of 'People' in the 'Systems Manual' section of System Builder.

10 Show Leadership

Are great leaders born or are they created? I don't know the answer to this question, but I do know that you can learn some of the leadership skills. I am sure there are many definitions of 'leadership', but to me it's all about taking and getting others to take action. In other words, you have got to do things and get others to do things. Things that both you and they WANT to do and all of which take your business towards its vision. There are quiet leaders and very noisy ones. They work in different places and it depends upon the people you are leading. There is a time and a place for everything and knowing when, is the key!

Leadership is all embracing and I would not attempt to analyse it too deeply here, but in 'showing leadership', you will, I believe, be inspirational, passionate and not afraid to take decisions, explain them to your employees and then take action! Measure the results and if things are not working, change things a bit until they do work.

Jim Collins, in his book 'Good to Great' talks about 'Level 5 leadership'. One of the many attributes of a level 5 leader is the ability, when things are going well, to attribute factors to others, rather than themselves. When things go poorly, however, they look in the mirror and blame themselves, taking full responsibility. How often as leaders, do we do the opposite?

HOW AVN CAN HELP

As with Team there are many resources available to help you in the realms of leadership, since great teams are formed from great leadership.

There's a recording of a presentation based on the book 'Good to Great' by Jim Collins in System Builder. Type in 'Good to Great' into the Knowledge base search.

There are many systems specifically designed around leadership in System Builder, accessed via the Systems Manual under the heading of 'Leadership'.

11 Be The Change You Want To See In Others

Too many people realise they want to change things in their business and as a result they want to change their people or their attitudes. The American business guru, Larry Winger, says "If your business is crap, it's because you are crap! If you have crap people, it's because you are crap at hiring them. If you have crap customers, it's because you are crap at selecting them" and so and so on. In other words, it's all down to you. If you want to change things you must change first. Once you do that you have some authority to change others. They will have seen the change in you and they will know you are serious about change. If they like it, they may be more amiable to change themselves. It's part of leadership, isn't it?

Making change permanent is not easily achieved. It depends upon a lot of things and in the end is down to how much desire you have to make the change.

I always remember Andy Gilbert (at the first AVN conference) talking about the whining dog! It's lying on the veranda whining away and another dog comes up and says "What's up?" The whining dog says "I'm lying on a nail." "Well, move," says the other dog and the whining dog replies "but it doesn't hurt enough!" That's the trouble with many of us. There has to be real pain in order to make it worthwhile changing. Of course, the reason for this is because it hurts to change. So, you are going to suffer more to start with than you would if you did nothing. We've all heard about 'lancing the boil'. You need to suffer some sharp pain in order for things to gradually improve. The problem then can be that as you move away from your problem, the pain diminishes and the need to continue the change process lessens. So what happens? You stop the changes and revert back to the old ways. I have come across so many businesses which have made that mistake. That's why the desire and belief for change has to be significant so that it becomes permanent. The best goals to have are where you move away from pain and start to gain. As the pain diminishes, the gain starts to increase. That keeps your incentive going!

12 Be Aware Of The Losers Trap

We've all tried things and thought 'Oh dear, this doesn't seem to be working'. Then we usually give up just before it starts to work. This is the 'losers trap'. When you start to change anything in business, nine times out of ten things get worse before they get better. If you have real belief in the process and know it's the right thing to do, then show leadership and stick with it. Not blindly of course. Constantly challenge the method and systems that you have introduced and look for a better way, but do not give in. It can be incredibly demotivating for your team if you are constantly starting something new and then giving in. We used to do this so often and then wondered why our team never trusted us. They used to look at us and say "They've been on another course. Give them until Friday and they will have forgotten it." And of course we did! As a result we were further away from our desired goals than ever. Worse still, we had again betrayed the team and not shown true leadership.

journey. We call these the quick wins and they help our members to keep noticing the benefits, both financially and emotionally, during this stage.

13 Know Who Does What

So often I go to see a business where there are multiple owners. Whether it's an incorporated business or not, it doesn't really matter. One of the first questions I ask will be "So who is the Managing Director/partner?" You know the answer I get. "Nobody!" Or they all say "I am." So who is the Finance Director? Who is the Marketing Director? Who is the Operations Director? Nobody knows. The most common failure in the accountancy business is – nobody knows who does what, and this also applies to the employees. They don't know either. They waste time doing things they need not or should not do and fail to do the things they should do. They then 'clog' up the business owner's time by asking them the same questions. It's a bit like children. They usually go to the parent who they think will give them the answer they want. If they don't get the right answer, they go to the other parent. It's just the same in business! Why? Because nobody has told them who does what and who is responsible. The alarming thing is that if they were advising their clients they would tell them to get clarity about 'who does what'.

I am sure you will have read Michael Gerber's 'E Myth Revisited'. If you have not, you should. In it he talks about business functions as 'boxes'. As a business owner you have to move out of one box and into another. Each time you do this, you systemise the function so that the work can be done by anyone and to the same high standard as you would do it. Okay, so that may not always be as practical as you would like, but the principle of defining the function and the role someone plays in it is a brilliant process to obtain the clarity needed. If you can do that in your business and work it throughout the entire business with all of your team, just imagine the clarity you will have. Think how much time would be saved by people simply knowing what they are supposed to do and who to approach when they have a problem.

So, for everyone, I would recommend that you define the 'roles and responsibilities'. Get them written down so there is total clarity and no confusion. Everyone here means 'everyone', so that includes business owners like you and your partners.

HOW AVN CAN HELP

At the AVN Masterclass we play Michael Gerber's DVD to the room because his message is crucially important. The System Builder software itself, initially developed back in 1999, was inspired by Michael Gerber's book and the philosophies have been core to its refinements and improvements over the years. System Builder allows you to define roles and allocate systems to those roles which can then be assigned to the individuals within your team.

14 If You Want To Be A Big Business Act Like A Big Business

When you ask a firm, "Do you have partner/Director's meetings?" they usually say "No, we are not really big enough to make it worthwhile!"

So, when is a business big enough to make it worthwhile? My opinion is that any business needs a formal process in place to analyse the results it's getting, consider strategies and make decisions. If you want to be a big business, act like a big business, even if you are currently small. Start and put into place systems, processes and procedures that big businesses would use and that will help your business become a big business. Even if you have regular meetings are they diarised on a monthly basis?

I ask partners how they arrange the dates of meetings. They usually say "Oh, we fix the date of the next meeting at the end of the current one." What happens? You usually find they cannot get a date for the next meeting because by then everybody has appointments or other commitments. So now it's six or eight weeks until the next meeting. This means things don't get done. Decisions get delayed and you are not moving towards your vision. How frustrating is that!

Have meeting dates fixed! Get them into everybody's diary months, and I mean months, ahead. I used to say "To infinity and beyond!" It tells others you mean business. It might even say it to you! It might be you have your meeting on the third Tuesday of every month or the fourth Monday, or whatever. It does not matter. What matters is the fact that everybody has a commitment to be at that meeting. They know when it is. They do not make appointments with clients for those times. Holidays are allowed, but not client work! It becomes 'the way we do business around here'.

HOW AVN CAN HELP
Type 'Board Meeting' into System Builder for specific help and guidance on running board meetings.

15 Make Decisions

It naturally follows that if you have a system in place which allows you to examine results and consider strategies (regular diarised meetings), you need to make and take decisions. You might think it obvious and it should be! However, how many business owners fail to do this? You would be amazed how many do not, or would you? Is yours one of those businesses which spend hours and hours examining all the facts? You know what you need to do, but to do it means making a decision which is not a nice one. It might upset somebody or worse still, you might have to get into an uncomfortable zone. So, what happens?

It usually gets put off to the next meeting. "Oh, we seem to have run out of time, so let's defer a decision to the next meeting when we will have more time!" How often does that happen?

Then at the next meeting you start all over again, trawling through all the facts, spending more valuable time going round and round in circles. At a meeting with some of the accountants I visit, I ask them how many times and how many hours they have spent discussing a particular issue? They give me the answer and suddenly they know they had spent too long and were prevaricating. Many decisions involve personal issues and we usually avoid personal issues if we can. This might be because they are seen to be confrontational and that is something that most people do not want to be, confrontational! Somebody, sometimes, has to be though. Grasp the nettle, bite the bullet, use whatever metaphor you want, but do something even if it's the wrong thing. At least you will find that out and know what the right thing is.

HOW AVN CAN HELP

Confrontation is incredibly difficult and highly avoided by many people. As such it can often lead to putting up with stuff for the sake of avoiding confrontation.

In the AVN Roadmap stage 4 there's a training workshop which includes understanding people and their characteristics. We're all very different and each of us have our strengths and weaknesses. The training includes mechanisms that can be applied to help overcome various weaknesses which can prevent progress in business. Dealing with confrontation is one example covered during the day.

16 And Then Take Action

Okay, you have made a decision. So, what's next? Do something! I know it sounds obvious and it is, but how many times do decisions get taken and then nothing happens?

Usually it's because nobody was charged with the task of taking the relevant action. The fact that a decision has been made usually means that everybody sighs with relief and before you know it, you've moved on to the next bit of business. Make somebody responsible. Make it clear that an outcome is required. Note I said outcome. That's what's important here. It's the result that really matters and as long as the action required to get the result is reasonable, you do not have to dictate the action. Let the person responsible decide that. But remember the timescale! The person responsible needs a timescale to work to so that at the very least they can report to the next meeting with the action taken and the outcome of that action.

HOW AVN CAN HELP

In System Builder there is a downloadable Action Plan template which you can use. This is it and it's something you can easily recreate using a word processor like Microsoft Word or Apple Pages. This is the template...

Action Planner

Winners take action, not just notes				
Action we will take	Priority	Who is going to do it?	When will it get done?	✓

Paper based action plans are convenient and tangible.

In our world of cloud based technology there's an abundance of cloud based action planning/task management tools available at your fingertips. Many are free for individuals and even small teams.

I personally recommend BaseCamp and Trello. They both perform similar functions. I've used both. Each allow you to very quickly log tasks during a meeting, assign them to individuals, set deadline dates and record progress. The beauty of using the cloud based apps is that if more than one person is interested in the task, comments, updates and progress information can be logged against the task as it's being progressed, so that information is available instantly negating the need for chasing for a progress update.

17 Hold One Another To Account (Or Get Someone Else To Do It)

This is all part of the process of taking decisions, taking action and then reporting on the outcome, the result. If you do not make people accountable for taking action, usually that action does not take place. It might in highly organised and motivated organisations, but usually that's not what we've got. We are aspiring to get there, but we are not there yet. So, we need to make people do things by making them accountable and when they don't, they need reminding of their responsibilities.

Partners or co-business owners are usually nice people. Very often they are friends. That's perfectly understandable isn't it! You are not likely to want to spend hours and hours of your life working with someone you hate. Strange if you do, but just because you are friends with someone (and it may not be friendship but merely respect), it does not mean that either you or they should not do what they are supposed to do.

> **HOW AVN CAN HELP**
> AVN host group accountability sessions using online video conferencing technology.
> These comprise of non-competing peers spread across the country as well as an AVN Practice Growth Expert. They're designed to help you progress through the roadmaps you're working on. This makes a good starting point and any additional roadmap or unrelated actions may be aired and discussed within the group with accountability for that action.

18 Have A 'Nasty Bastard' On Your Board!

Having a Non-Executive Director in your partner/ Director meetings can be priceless. That person can be the one who really helps you take the hard decisions and then holds you and others to account. Even if you do not wish to challenge your partner or partners, they can. They don't have anything to lose except your respect if they don't do it! Because they are not involved in the 'day to day' stuff, they do not get involved in any politics. They see things from another perspective. A different perspective! They can ask the awkward questions and not worry. They can even ask stupid questions because they do not have the answers. They do **not** need to have them. You do! If you cannot satisfy them that it's the correct thing to do, in all probability you will convince yourselves that it's not the correct thing to do.

I know many accountancy businesses now employing this process in assisting them in their businesses. It works brilliantly. It takes brave people though to allow a third party into their business and play this role. It is opening them up to be challenged and that's not easy. However, the rewards for those that do this are immense.

19 Use Common Sense

If it seems sensible, it probably is. Sometimes I think we all lose sight of one of the greatest gifts we were ever given. Common sense! Far too often we make life and work too complicated. It's like an illness. We fail to see the blindingly obvious, only to get lost in a mist of complications. There always has to be a more complicated answer! One of the lecturers at Durham Business School said that most of the stuff he talked about was 'common sense, but not commonly used'. How true that is. All the stuff in this book, if you think about it, is common sense, but not commonly used. That's because it's not always easy to apply.

Business is simple, but not easy. The principles are very simple when you think about it. You have an idea, either to provide goods or services, and off you go. You may need some components so you need to buy stuff in. Oh yes, and you need to have some premises to operate from. You start to need people to help you deliver some of these goods or services and before you know it you are off into a world of bureaucracy and intrigue. People need managing and the customers need servicing. It's all so time consuming and you seem to have to do it all! It seemed such a simple idea at the outset and it has now got all complicated. So, when life is complicated, remember to keep things as simple as you can, when you can and remember, use common sense wherever you can.

20 Knowing The Right Questions Can Be More Important Than Having The Right Answers

I learnt some time ago that having great questions was more important than having all the answers. You usually find that others have the answers. You don't need to. You just need to know the questions to ask. That's why a Non-Executive on your Board or in your meetings is so valuable. They know all the questions to ask. The problem is that from my experience most accountants, (it must have been the training they have had), always want to know all the answers! They cannot seem to ever admit that they don't. When a client asks a question, you rarely hear an accountant say "Oh, I don't know the answer to that. I will find out for you and get back. Is that okay?" Many have this need to find a solution straight away because they think that is what their client expects.

Train yourself to think more in terms of having a bank of great questions to ask a client. Having great questions enables you to see issues differently. You may have an answer, but don't worry if you don't, because you can bet that someone else will. That someone may well be your client who is now thanking you for asking such a great question.

21 Build A Great Team Around You

Building a great team is possibly one of the most significant factors in creating a successful business. So how do you build a great team? Once you have got a great team, how do you keep it great? We have talked already about **Leadership, Management People Skills** and the need to show **Passion.** Certainly, these three areas of business are critical in helping to build a great team, but there are plenty of others.

If you are starting from scratch, it is worth remembering some of the following points. If you have 'staff' and want to create a 'team culture' you may want to think about them as well.

In 1998 HGH had a culture, but it was the wrong culture. We had no leadership and there was a 'them and us' type attitude. I believe that the key to success is all around the word 'communication.' It is the key. Communicate with total clarity and please remember to be consistent.

HOW AVN CAN HELP
I've already made reference to team building resources and
training available through AVN.
AVN Roadmap stage 4 focuses heavily in building a great team
and developing the culture through its programme and
training workshops.

22 Communicate

Some people are naturally good at communicating.
Others need to skill up and have systems to help them. Even
those who are good need help sometimes. The thing is, we need
to remember that it's a two-way process. You need to listen
better as well as talk! God gave us two ears and one mouth and
perhaps we should use them in direct proportion. Even when we
listen, do we really hear? I remember saying to people at HGH
that we have an open door policy. Yes, we did. Our doors were
open unless we were in a meeting with clients or a private
meeting with partners or other team members. However, just
because our doors were open did not mean that we actually
practiced the art of listening. Someone had a problem and they
wanted to tell me about it. Yes, of course they could tell me, but
wait a minute, I have to be at that meeting in an hour and I am
already running late. Yes, go on tell me, what's your problem?
The thing is I was pretending to listen, but I was not hearing
anything. My mind was elsewhere and yet the person I was
listening to thought I was genuinely caring about their problem.
They trusted me and yet I was betraying them and not really
caring at all. I did not feel as if I was betraying anyone, but it was
just that I was really busy.

Now I know you will say, "I have never done that," but I bet you
will have at some time and never even noticed. It's best to have a
'closed door' policy, but to let them open it and for you to really
listen and hear what people say. Make time to listen. Have it as
part of your systems. Some people say that they manage their

businesses by walking around and talking and listening on a daily basis. That way they get to understand the issues which are affecting their team and can react to them before they become critical.

In any accountancy business it is important for people to know what's going on. The day to day things that affect the running of the business like knowing where people are. How many times have you called a colleague or gone to someone's office, only to find they are out, they are on an audit or a course and you had either forgotten or nobody had told you? Sometimes clients come into the office and if only you had known you could have asked them for that bit of missing information or that last question. You might have even won a new client, but nobody else in the building knows that, so when they ring to ask for you, reception has no idea who they are! That looks really good, doesn't it? This is why you need systems to tell people what's happening.

We had a simple weekly system and we called it 'team brief'. We had a template with headings such as...

- Accounting Jobs in to Start
- Appointments with Potential Clients
- Results of Potential Client Appointments
- Clients Lost and Why?
- Product Sales
- Customer Complaints
- Internal Complaints
- Information Relevant to Clients
- Thanks from
- Thanks to
- Training Courses (Tuesday-Monday)
- Audits to be Attended (Tuesday-Monday)
- Health & Safety Issues
- Visitors Expected
- Birthdays
- Social Events
- Any Other Business

A member of our team was responsible for issuing the blank template via email. Everyone completed what they could and sent it back. The team member collated all the data and then fired it back out to all the team. Everybody had all the details as to who was where and when and which clients might be calling at the office and when, who were the new clients and so on and so on.

The partners met monthly (the same day every month) for their partner's meetings. We had all the client managers meet the partners before the partner's meeting. We had all the focus group chairpersons meet before the manager's meetings (all on the same day). This way any issues arising from those two meetings could be addressed in the partner's meetings. Now you may say 'there's nothing clever about any of this', and you would be right, but how many accountants meet systematically? All this helps create good communications and good communications helps a business achieve its goals.

HOW AVN CAN HELP
There are additional meeting agenda templates available in System Builder from which you can develop a version to suit your own preferences. These are best accessed through the People section of the Systems Manual.

23 Communicate With Clarity

Very often we say we have told someone what we want or we say things like "I told you this before." Very often that is true. We have! But the person we have told has either not heard what we have said or they heard something else! In larger organisations it is difficult to get one message across to a number of people and the danger is that we tell individuals what we wanted to tell everybody. Guess what? They all hear a different message. You find yourself thinking 'I didn't say that'. Chances are, you didn't. It's just that somebody heard it!

They heard it because that's what they wanted to hear or you did not communicate with clarity. Now I think I am a realist. You will never get ten people all to hear the same story and all get exactly the same message at the same time. Life is not like that, but it does help if you take these tips.

When trying to tell a story to a number of people, always try to tell all of them at the same time. Yes, it's obvious I know, but how many of us actually do this. We go around telling people individually or in groups. Never tell them on a one to one basis. Even with a script you are likely to deviate and they will tend to hear different things. Result, confusion! When talking to a group, use scripts whenever you can. Never rely on 'winging it'. Rehearse your presentation. Never make the mistake of saying to a colleague, "You speak to Bill and I'll have a word with Mary." I can guarantee that Bill will hear a different story to Mary, probably because he has been told a different one!

This is what I mean about having clarity. It is so easy for people to get confusing messages. You don't need to help them! You have to be as precise as you can and be systematic in the way you communicate so that people hear the same thing, understand the same thing and most importantly, for the outcome to be the same.

24 Communicate With Consistency

Next challenge! How many times have you been told, "You are just not consistent?" Well, actually you are lucky if you have been told this. Most of us are just inconsistent and nobody has the courage to tell us! You see it is linked to the 'clarity thing'. We need to keep on delivering the same message day after day! We need to set out the rules and play by them day after day. Not keep changing them. This is not to say that things cannot change. Of course they can, but it's better to see the change as a change in emphasis than a change in direction. The worst inconsistency is that we set out a strategy on Monday and have forgotten it by Friday! No consistency at all. The worst thing is that every time you do this, the trust with your team is broken, yet again, and they are less inclined to believe (hear) what you say in the future. What's the point, they will say, it never happens!

In order to get consistency into your communication process – systemise it. Make sure you have meeting dates diarised for infinity. They are part of how you run your business!

> **HOW AVN CAN HELP**
> System Builder is AVN's systems tool we provide to AVN members to help them systemise their accountancy practice and allow AVN members to resell System Builder to their clients when helping them systemise their businesses. System Builder comes with 'ready to tweak' systems for an accountancy practice and 'ready to tweak' systems for any business. (These simply don't include operational whereas the accountancy practice ones do).
> Utilising the Board meeting systems and the team meeting systems is a great place to start systemising your practice.

25 Remember 'The Emotional Bank Account'

Like any bank account, before you can make a withdrawal, you need to have something in the account, meaning you need to have made some deposits. Yes, I know you can get an overdraft, but with people's emotions being overdrawn is the last place to be. Every time you do something good for a person, you put something into the account. If you keep on building the trust and they are happy with you, the account gets fuller and fuller. Okay, so one day you make a blunder and it goes wrong! What happens? Well, it depends.

If you have a lot in the emotional bank account and there is a withdrawal, there is still something left. Of course it depends upon the blunder as to how much is withdrawn. But the fact that there is enough there to withstand the withdrawal is what matters. We all make mistakes. It is what makes us humans and not machines.

We need to build up a large balance in the accounts of our team. This creates trust in the relationship. Of course it works both ways and you may find it helpful to explain this principle to them, as well as understanding it yourself.

It also works with your customers! Things go wrong when you work with them. The bigger the bank account, the more likely they are to forgive you, particularly if you correct the error quickly and to their total satisfaction.

26 Speed Stuns

As I said, things go wrong. It is part of life's rich pattern. It is what you do next that matters. Putting a problem right is a great opportunity to make a brilliant impression in the mind of the wronged party. Putting it right quickly stuns and most people will love you more than they would have if you had done it right in the first place.

I remember a story I heard whilst at Durham Business School. There was a firm of garden machinery retailers who actually sent out faulty equipment! Not faulty so as to be a danger, but annoying enough to get the buyer to make a complaint by ringing them up. They would then immediately send a person out to rectify the problem. Guess what! The customers thought they were brilliant and would be a walking and talking testimonial for them. Whether this story is accurate I am not sure, but it does demonstrate the point about putting problems right and doing it quickly.

Think about this. We have all experienced things that go wrong. How impressed are we when the supplier puts it right, to our total satisfaction and they do it quickly! How likely are we to talk about them and to talk in a positive way?

27 Under-Promise And Over Deliver

Yes, speed stuns but how annoying is it when someone says "We can do it by Friday," and it's three weeks on Tuesday before they do it! Isn't it a great surprise, and a nice one, when you are told it will be done by Friday and it gets done by Thursday! Far too many people promise and cannot deliver. So simply put, never promise on something you cannot deliver. Better still, manage the expectations of your customer by saying when it will be done, and then do it quicker than the date you gave.

28 Disciples And Terrorists

We all have them! You know who they are! But do you do anything about them? You know your disciples. They are always on your side even if they question what you wish them to do. They are enthusiastic, they will go the extra mile and stay behind to get the job done. You know your terrorists. They are nice to your face and shoot you behind your back. You leave the room and they say poisonous things about you and the business. They tell others, "It won't work, you know it won't. It is a waste of time." On my visits to many accountancy businesses, I have asked the question, "How many people do you currently employ who you would not re-employ?" The response is amazing. Usually you can see them counting the fingers on one hand and sometimes its two hands! When there is more than one business owner, they usually have different people on the fingers! The next easy question is of course to ask them, "So why are you currently employing them?" You never get a satisfactory answer. They usually look at one another in a despairing sort of way.

So what should you do? Simply put, you should reward your disciples and manage your terrorists out of the door. Rewarding your disciples and keeping them engaged is not difficult. Managing your terrorists out of the door is not easy. However, it can and should be done.

But I can hear you say 'Yes, but it is so difficult to remove poor performing people, what with all the employment legislation and everything.' It is, but it can and should be done. This may all seem a bit draconian! I am not advocating you go around with a big stick beating people up, but you should manage people. It is what they expect. This may even be part of the problem. Managing people is part of being a leader and it is necessary to run and become a successful business.

So, you have someone who is a terrorist. What should you do? Firstly, do you have an honest and open relationship with this person? I don't mean you have to like them. It helps but it is not always necessary. Have you discussed with them why they are being a terrorist? Many times this doesn't happen. I was guilty of it sometimes. It was confrontational to have a conversation around this topic and most of us do not want to be confrontational, least of all me. I would ignore the problem and hope it would go away or someone else might address it. It did not go away and of course no one else addressed it. When I actually sat down and talked to them about my concerns, sometimes I actually understood what it was which made them behave in that way and we were able to do something about it. Problem nearly solved! However, you need to then monitor future behaviour and build on the trust you have started to create. Continuing conversations were the key here. It was all about understanding the issues behind the behaviour.

However, it doesn't always work out that way. You talk and you get nowhere! You recognise that despite your very best efforts things are just not going to change and really this person should be elsewhere. They may actually see that for themselves. If you really believe you are not going to make any progress you need to get some good advice from an employment law specialist. Start to manage the person. Agree performance targets with them. You should have them anyway (see idea 50) and monitor their performance. It is not difficult, but it does take discipline and time. You then measure the performance and are able to manage them better. It may be that this process will make the individual want to seek alternative employment. If not, it does give you the appropriate information upon which to take the relevant action as advised by the employment law specialists.

I have worked with some accountants who just never seem to take any action. They talk endlessly about the problem and then never do anything. They spend hours addressing the issue at each partner meeting and then conclude 'It's is too difficult to do anything about it, so let's just leave it'. The problem does not go away, but instead just gets worse. When we applied for IIP, an initial survey of our team was carried out. The assessor concluded that there were three people in our organisation who were, as she put it, 'bad apples'. She said, "I am not supposed to say this, but you need to get rid of them before they infect the others."

The funny thing is that when we had removed them, the others said that it was about time we had taken that action! They actually thanked us! We had shown leadership and done something. The atmosphere in the office changed overnight. It was another significant change in the culture of the business.

So why do we persist with putting up with things that we know are not right?

29 Select Your Image And Identify Your Ideal Client

Does an image matter? More specifically, does yours? I believe it does. Why? Well, you cannot be all things to all people. It is a well-known fact. It is an expression we have all heard and we usually accept as being correct. So why do most accountants try to be all things to all comers? If they walk through the door, we grab them and as long as we think they will pay our fees, we do work for them.

This is where your image comes in. If you want to create a type of business that attracts the type of clients you want, you need to have an image which the ideal client will recognise as being 'what they want' as well. This is why it is important for you to identify the type of client you want. I am not suggesting you would not work for any other type of client, but you would and should only spend time and money marketing to the ideal client. If someone else walks through your door and you happen to like them and the possibility of working with them, then you can, it is your choice. When I was a sole practitioner I used to say that I was a specialist at being a 'general practitioner'. If that is what you want, that's fine. But in today's market I believe you need to be clear in your own mind as to the type of work and people you want to work with in order for your business to be really successful.

HOW AVN CAN HELP
In System Builder there's a resource called 'Ideal Customer.'
Use this to help you. We take you through this process in AVN
Roadmap stage 2.

30 Decide Upon Your Pricing Policy

Setting your pricing policy is part of creating your image and defining your ideal customer. Are you going to be cheap and cheerful or expensive and exclusive? Or are you going to be somewhere in between? You cannot be both, but you could be somewhere in between. Do you want to have the Managing Director of your £20 million turnover client sitting in the reception with your subcontractor client who is covered in plaster and who is straight off the building site? I am not saying that there is anything wrong either with him or as having him as a client, but the truth is that neither will feel comfortable in one another's company. It's a simple fact of life and you need to understand that. Determining your prices is part of the filtering process of who you do work with.

I know that some businesses have had their cake and they have eaten it! They have opened another office somewhere else to deal with the smaller clients, offering a cheap and cheerful approach and their larger, perhaps their more demanding clients are kept separate. This can work but you must be careful and run them as completely separate businesses and create a separate image and 'brand'. Most however do not do this, but decide in advance what they want to be and who they want to work with.

successfully value price rather than price competitively. We also provide pricing software called 'Time's Up', which is specifically designed for accountants. It helps you value price your full range of services from basic compliance through to business advisory work, complemented with professional brochures which help you package your services in a professional and impressive way that sets you apart from the competition.

31 Remember, What You Can Measure You Can Manage

Yes, this is another of those slick expressions somebody has thought of. But, it is true. Having targets we can measure does help things get done. Anyway, if you don't know what you are aiming at, i.e. a target, anything might happen, least of all, what you wanted to happen.

Andy Gilbert talks about having auditable goals. If you want to achieve something, how do you, and anybody else for that matter, know when you have achieved it? It must be measurable! The process to achieving what you wanted is also improved if you set goals along the way. Sometimes the process is a long one and just to have an end target is too far away. It helps to break it down into smaller goals.

Anyway, achieving a goal is an opportunity to celebrate success and that's a great way of motivating your team and yourself!

HOW AVN CAN HELP
This is mentioned later in this book, so I won't go into too much detail right now but AVN's OnePage Plan™ is a great tool to help you achieve this.

32 Have Fun In The Workplace

Accountancy businesses are thought to be a bit serious. John Cleese, of Monty Python fame, created a picture of accountants who were dull and boring. Some are, but the vast majority of those I have met, are not. But sometimes the work and the working environment can be a bit dull. Why? It does not have to be. Now I am not saying that you must go around telling jokes all day, but why not think of as many ways, better still, get your team to think of as many ways to make work, more fun. I know accountancy businesses that have games in reception, games rooms and gymnasiums. They don't spend all their time playing games, but they do encourage their team and themselves to lighten up a little whenever the opportunity arises.

Stephen Covey talks about the 'seventh habit'. He calls it 'sharpening the saw'. This is exactly the kind of thing he means. When you have fun and relax, you are relaxing the mind and this helps you to concentrate on the important stuff!

HOW AVN CAN HELP
We run a workshop that helps you develop the culture of your team and help you better understand how developing a culture that's a fun environment, fun with a serious intent, can help you improve productivity and financial performance. We provide many ideas that are proven to be effective in accountancy practices today.

33 But Be Serious About Serious Stuff

Yes, you need to be serious when you need to be serious! Accountancy tends to be a serious business. After all, no business person I know of wants their accountant to be a bit of a joke, but a sense of humour in the right place always helps.

Creating the correct impression is critical and as you know, you only get one opportunity to create the correct impression. Being serious at the right time is critical.

I often get asked about the different dress codes that accountants operate in their businesses. There was a 'fashion' not so long ago to dress down and allow smart casual clothing. This seems to have changed and most of the accountants I visit (but not all) have reverted to the more formal collar and tie. Some, and I think this is an interesting point, dress for the occasion. If they are with clients they will dress accordingly. If not, then smart will do! Other firms have opted for a corporate dress code. This can be a powerful message to existing and potential clients. It also helps with the image you are trying to create.

Does any of this matter? Well, I think it does. I feel that all clients expect their accountants to look professional. Part of that is creating the right impression and being serious when you need to be serious.

34 Empower Your Team

Empowerment is a much used and overly complicated way of expressing the point that you should involve your team in your business as much as you can.

Earlier I wrote about managing people and how sometimes we fail to do that. We abrogate responsibility and then wonder why things don't work. I am not suggesting that by 'empowering people' you are not going to have to manage them. People sometimes refer to a self-managed team! Fine, but they only work because the team has clearly defined goals which links to the overall business objectives/goals and they measure their progress in achieving those goals. That process needs managing and someone has to do it! Anyway, everyone needs to be accountable to someone and that process is about managing people.

So why involve your team in your business? Well, I believe and others do too, that if you get your team to take responsibility for the things they do, and for getting things done and for them to take initiatives at the same time, you are more likely to be successful. How can you do this? Read on!

Empowering your people also means allowing them to make decisions and take action.

I heard a great story about a man who filled his car up at a filling station. There was a fault with the pump and it spilled diesel all over his shoes. When he went to pay, he complained (politely of course) to the attendant and said the pump needed attention. The attendant immediately asked the man how much his shoes cost. The man told him and when he had filled in a simple form, the attendant gave him £54 to compensate him and replace the spoiled shoes. Wow! Can you imagine the delight on the face of the motorist? The attendant told him he was authorised in the event of a real problem to compensate a customer up to a maximum of £100. No silly calls and delays to get a result. How impressed was the customer? Very! How impressed would you be in similar circumstances?

HOW AVN CAN HELP
Type 'initiative' into System Builder. This will reveal a short video about how to encourage your team to take the initiative.

35 Involve Your Team

We talked a bit about 'empowerment' and my definition of what that means. We looked at why it was important but we did not discuss how we could do it. Much of what I talk about now, I learnt from Graham Lamont. When Graham worked with HGH in 1999/2000 we were endeavouring to change our business. I have already said we were lacking leadership and profits. We had a poor culture. It was the bosses and the staff. If we talked about 'our team' it was a joke. We did not mean it and frankly we were embarrassed to use the word because it sounded too American! A bit evangelical!

Graham talked to us about many things around how we could change and how we could develop a team culture. He talked about setting up Focus Groups in the business and how these would work. Now I know many of us don't like the words 'focus groups'; they were words associated with the late eighties and early nineties and political parties. If you feel strongly about that, and I do a bit, then call them something else, but do consider using them in your business. Why? Because they work! They worked at HGH and I know many other firms who have used them in their business and they have worked there as well.

So what are focus groups, what do they do and how are you supposed to make them work? Well, I can only tell you about my experiences and how we did it.

They were a system of getting people together to assist with key aspects of 'the how'. We had developed our vision of the business. We had debated the core mission of our business for some time and from that we had developed the key strategies (tactics) of how we were going to get to where we wanted to be. This may sound very simple, but it was not of course. However, we did get eventual clarity as to what the 'how's' were, but we needed everyone to be involved in their delivery. We, as business owners, could not do it all and even if we could, was it wise to do it all? No, we needed our 'team' as they were to become, to help in the process. If they believed in where we were going and understood and wanted to help in the 'how we were going to get there' we knew we would be more likely to achieve our ultimate goals and achieve our vision.

Graham talked to us about five key areas where he believed our team could seriously help in achieving our business vision. These were in:

1. Marketing.
2. Customer services.
3. New products and services.
4. Systemising the business.
5. Developing a culture of lifetime learning.

I guess that the first four might be obvious, but the last one not so. We will look at each one in turn, but start by looking at how you might run them in your business.

HOW AVN CAN HELP
In System Builder there's a guide you can follow to run an event which will help you get your team on board. Type in 'Let's get going' into System Builder to find it.

36 Focus Groups (Or Whatever You Wish To Call Them)

How do you run them? Well, we had our meetings on the third Monday of every month with the exception of December and the month we had our 'celebration day' (idea number 43). So, we had ten a year. The five groups met on the same day but not all at the same time, for reasons that will become apparent. They started at about 9.00am and each meeting could last up to an hour and a half but no longer. They could be shorter, that did not matter, but no longer. We explained the rationale behind focus groups to all our team and asked them to select two groups they would like to join. We asked them to weight their requests, saying that we would guarantee them their first choice, but not necessarily their second.

At the first meetings of each group a chairperson and a vice-chairperson were elected. There was also someone who would take the minutes of the meeting. Graham suggested to us that this should be someone from another group so that they need not worry about their contribution but just concentrate on taking the minutes. After a while they also used to join in on the meetings! The minutes of all the meetings were circulated to all the team to enable them to know what was going on in other groups.

At this time there were five partners at HGH. Each partner also selected two focus groups, but they sat on the groups as 'policy advisers' rather than partners! This was very difficult, particularly to start with, as it meant we had a sharp learning curve in letting our people move things on without interference from ourselves. Why were we 'policy advisers?' As partners, we decided that if one of the group came up with a suggestion that would assist in the strategies we had agreed upon, then the two partners on that group had the authority to bind the others by making a decision in that meeting to either go with the suggestions or explain why in their opinion they would need to consult the others. This had the effect of speeding up the decision-making process and had a dramatic effect on the team members within that group. They felt things were moving and that they were actually influencing the business. And of course they were.

Did they work right from the start? No, they certainly did not. Did everybody take part in them? No, they did not. Initially they were a 'forum for complaints.' Most of the comments were negative. Things like the state of the decorations in the ladies loos and the fact that the kitchen needed a new kettle seemed to take precedence over the more important matters! But when we reflected, were they more important? If the ladies loos did need redecoration and the kitchen a new kettle, they were important issues and previously there was no way of people actually communicating that to the business owners.

After a while these issues were resolved. Things did get done, even if initially they were thought to be small. People in the groups knew that they were having an input. They started to believe in the process and trust it more and they took more of an active role

A few words of warning!

1. You may need to carefully manage who is elected as your chairpersons. You don't want a terrorist as a chairperson. In all honesty that is not likely, but you do need to make sure this does not happen. Perhaps speak to someone who you would like to do the job and see if they might be interested. They may not have the confidence and you may need to reassure them. Is this devious? Perhaps, but it is eventually going to get you what you want!

2. You have to believe in the concept of focus groups! If you just like the idea but are not sure it will work, then don't bother with them at all. If you believe in them, **make them work**. I have been to many firms which have tried them and they say they did not work. When I asked them how long had they had been running them the typical answer was 'about three months'. It took us at HGH about 18 months to really see the benefits come through and for the culture in the business to start to change. All of the partners/Directors must believe in them and actively be seen to support them. It is no good one saying he does not mind the others doing them or just turning up for meetings when he/she felt like it. Everybody needs to show commitment to them! We had a simple philosophy.
    The only reason you were excused attending a meeting was because you were on holiday (which was totally acceptable) or because you were dead! (which was unfortunate!)

Let us now take a look at the five main areas and consider in more detail the benefits of each for your business.

37 Involve Your Team In Marketing

The main problem is most people say, "I know nothing about marketing and how can I help to market the business?" I think it is often easier to start and explain to everybody that, everything we all do, actively markets the business. We may not realise it, but it does! Everybody's behaviour says something about the place we work. Can you imagine a client being in a wine bar on a Friday night? They are having a quiet drink with their partner and one of your team is drunk on the floor. Firstly, what does that say to them about your team member and secondly what does that say about your business? You employ that person! All this may seem extreme, but I assure you it is very relevant. Getting everybody to be aware of these small things is critical to your overall success. The behaviour and attitude of you and your team tells your clients and potential clients many things about your business.

I would suggest that the purpose of this group is to think of ideas and take action on them regarding how to market your existing and new products and services to both existing and new clients. If this seems a bit vague, think about it! Does everybody in your business, and that includes you, know with total certainty about all the existing products and services you could sell now? I doubt it. If you did, how many of those services are you selling and who are you selling them to? Having a group of people coming together and going through a process of clarification on these things alone can be very effective. Producing a list of all services and then finding out who buys what enables you to sell more services! Remember the golden rule – it is better to sell more to your existing clients than to try and gain new clients. It is a lot cheaper! I have heard many people say "the best customer you have is the one you currently have" and I guess that is true, provided it is a customer you want!

You will recall that when you created your vision for the

business, you worked out the 'ideal client'. How many of those do you have? Have you graded your clients? If not, who should do it? How should you grade them? What are you going to do with the results? So many questions! Having your marketing group will help sort these out and help allocate responsibility for the tasks

Getting new clients by referrals from existing clients is the best and cheapest way of acquiring new business. How are you going to get referrals and who is going to get them? Who is going to manage the process? Who will measure the results? Another positive marketing method is to systematically ask for testimonials. Who is going to do this and how are you going to look after and use those you get? You can see that there are lots of simple and practical things that others can do and would want to do. Having a structure such as this enables others to take responsibility and to be accountable.

At HGH we had no brochures. Now I know that not everybody likes brochures, but we did a lot of telemarketing and we had little to leave with the prospect. Our groups compiled the content of our brochure. Their knowledge about the services we could provide was improved immeasurably, their confidence improved and they felt proud and totally involved in the process. They were involved in all the other things I have referred to above and they knew they were contributing to the growth in the business and taking it towards the vision we had all created!

HOW AVN CAN HELP
There are some 'ready to tweak' brochures available for you in System Builder – the Cloud Accounting Services and the Business Consulting Services are a couple of examples. You can use these as they are or modify them as you see fit and then have them produced by your graphic designer, including testimonials and case studies you've collected.
Service request sheets act as great aid memoires for you and your team when talking to prospects and clients about the services you can offer.

There are many 'ready to tweak' marketing systems in System
Builder that you can involve your team with straight away.
Access these via the Systems Manual section.

Type 'woo' into the System Builder knowledge base and you
will find the Windows of Opportunity chart which helps you
identify the services you told your clients about and have sold
to your clients. Telling clients about your services regularly is a
great exercise which reminds your clients about how you can
better serve them and of course leads to additional work for
you.

There are many more examples I can give in this area where
AVN can help. Talk to your Practice Improvement Expert to
learn about these and events we run in this area.

38 Involve Your Team In Customer Services

Customer care! Where do I start? This area is, I think,
the easiest and yet perhaps the most difficult area to handle.
Done brilliantly it can transform your business. Done badly it
can ruin it! So many people talk about the importance of great
customer care, but then do nothing to deliver it.

Let's start with my definition of great customer care and the
purpose of this group. I believe it is to 'deliver on a consistent
basis an outstanding experience at every point of contact with
everybody our business had any contact with'.

As you can see, my definition was not exclusively for clients, but
everybody. Why? Well, how can you be brilliant with a customer
but appalling with a supplier? If you want an exceptional
culture in your business it must be like the stick of rock and
have the writing right the way through it. Anyway, that supplier
might become a client one day, particularly if they are so
impressed by their experience of working with you.

I believe that everyone your business comes into contact with needs to experience things which makes them talk to others. They need to be in awe of you. I know many books have been written on this whole area of customer services and it is not my intention to do so, but there are some golden grains I would like to include here which although common sense things, are very often not commonly applied.

When you make a telephone call, how impressed are you if it is answered within three rings? A bright, cheerful person answers the phone, tells you the name of their business and gives their name and asks how can they help you? Sounds simple, doesn't it? But it will not happen unless someone makes it happen. Who is going to do this and what is your firm's script?

When people come to see you in your offices how are they greeted? When they walk through the door, does your receptionist even know who they are? Can they get through your doors without having to negotiate far too many buttons? Have you got clear signage? Are they offered refreshments? Are they offered the loos? Is your reception warm and comforting and is there interesting literature for them to read whilst waiting to see you? Does it look like an old fashioned dentist's waiting room or a cosy hotel lobby? Are your offices as smart and as comfortable as your own home? These are just some of the things which many do not treat with importance. And they are important. Would these things astound a client? I think not, so they should be a 'given'. Getting these things right are only the building blocks to stunning customer services, but there is little point in trying something really clever if you cannot get the basics right.

In what other ways can you stun a client? How can you really amaze them? Do you have all the answers? You may have some but I guess your team will have many more. If they have the ideas, is it quite likely they will carry them out rather than if they were yours? You know the answer as all of us like our own ideas the best and we usually follow through on them. This is why if you have a group from your team focussing on all these and thinking of many others, over time you are likely to develop stunning customer services.

I often tell the story of my visit to the AVN member, Clear Vision, in Corsham in Wiltshire. Having arranged by telephone to see them, within ten minutes I received an email giving confirmation of the visit and a link to a map of their location. A day before my visit I received another email saying they were really looking forward to seeing me and if I had any queries or should I encounter any problems on my journey I was to ring them and they would do all they could to assist me. I arrived on the due date to find a notice in the car park saying that I had a reserved space. I parked my car and walked to their entrance to find there was a red carpet along the pavement to the front door! Yes, there was a red carpet! Just for me! I walked into their well-lit, comfortable reception to be greeted by a cheerful voice which said "You must be Jonathan Holroyd. It is lovely to meet you. Have you had a good journey? Would you like to look at our drinks menu? Do you need to freshen up? Can I look after your mobile phone while you are here with us? I can log the calls and give you a list when you leave. That way you won't have to catch up on any missing calls." She also asked whether she could look after my car keys as they had a stationery delivery that day and they might have to move my car if the wagon could not get around the corner. It wasn't all as direct as that but was built into a conversation. However, nothing was missed. I also recall that in the reception they had cartoon caricatures of all the team! This was both different and a talking point. I was taken with my Columbian coffee (by the way, the drinks menu also included bottled beer and champagne by the glass) to their waiting area. There was a jukebox in the corner and a glass of tokens to use to to play your favourite record. In the room there was also a glass-fronted fridge, just to show you that they did actually have beer and champagne!

I had my meeting with Rob, said my goodbyes and was given my car keys and telephone (nobody had called me). I was also escorted to my car to find that it was full of helium balloons and there was a bottle of champagne on the front seat. Even more stunning though, was a small gold box, the size of a ring box, on the dashboard. It had a ribbon around it and inside was £4.20, which was the exact toll fee across the bridge into Wales. You see, they knew where I was going after I left them because they had asked me!

I asked myself that if I had been a prospective client of that business, would I have been impressed and would I have been more or less likely to have chosen to do business with them? I think you know the answer. Am I suggesting that these things are right for your business? Not necessarily but I bet many would be. Anyway, what other things could your business do to impress both existing and new customers? How are you going to develop these ideas and who is going to carry them out? Answer, your focus group dedicated to developing stunning customer services.

HOW AVN CAN HELP
Type 'telephone' into System Builder and access the 'Answering the Telephone' system. Also there's a great system for visitors to the office. Both of these systems help you create a great first impression.
Also in System Builder there's a resource called 'Wow How' (search for that). This helps you identify many great ways to continually wow your prospects and customers both in terms of first impressions and ongoing in every single interaction.
Roadmap stage 3 includes wow'ing your customers too.

39 Involve Your Team In New Product And Services

If you are an AVN member you will have more services/products than you can possibly handle. I say that firstly because it is probably true, and secondly involving your team in their delivery will take away some of the strain from having to do it yourself. Anyway, having your team understand the tools and resources will be paramount to your success in using them. It does not have to be AVN stuff either.

In our Innovations Focus Group we had a gentleman called John Hancox. John did the quarterly VAT for a cash business, a mini-mart. It was a simple analysed spreadsheet which he then coded up to produce the annual accounts. He suggested to the group that if he was allocated some time he could develop this further. He then said that this could be sold to other clients who had poor records and who wanted to make their own lives easier. He even said that as a result of better records perhaps we would improve the under recovery we had with them and they might become profitable clients! By the end of 2002 we had sold John's simple software tool to 79 clients. We charged them £250 for the software and a further £200 for training and support. He was right. Most of them became more profitable to us as the under recovery reduced and in some cases became an over recovery.

Getting back to the AVN stuff! Many of our team did not know enough about the resources and tools, and became more familiar with them through the focus group. Decisions were made as to which we felt would be the best ones to roll out to our clients. The marketing group were involved in the process of how and training was given to those who wanted to develop the skills and to actually deliver the stuff. This took away some of the responsibility of the partners and freed up some of our time. People were beginning to take responsibility!

HOW AVN CAN HELP
There are service information sheets in System Builder. Use these to decide which services you want to offer (at least for now) and use them also to train your team.

40 Involve Your Team In Systemising Your Business

If you have ever read Michael Gerber's book 'The E Myth' you will have read his message about the relevance of 'systemisation' in a successful business. We all recognise that nobody does things as well as we can do it ourselves! It is a recognised fact! If we have systems that people can follow, just, maybe just, they will be able to because they can follow the system and do it just like we would do it. This may seem a bit flippant but actually it is not. Doing something well is not difficult, particularly if you know what enables it to be done well and it is consistently done that way. The word 'consistently' is important here. I glibly used to say that we should be consistent, even if we were consistently wrong. At least people would know what they were getting. There is nothing worse than getting it right and then getting it wrong – consistently! People never know where they are with you. Systems allow your people to deliver a high level of performance and to do it on a consistent basis.

More specifically, if you are partners who tend to do things your own way then surely you must recognise the 'all firm benefits' of doing it 'one way'. Your team will, even if you don't. Our systems focus group set about standardising the way we did things at HGH. From standard letters to standardising working papers files to standard procedures as to how we prepared accounts and what we did and what we did not do throughout the practice. We created a conveyor belt approach to this work because we knew it was the way to make some of our work more profitable. For some it was the only way. For the other work it became even more profitable. Our team were happier because they did not have to think, 'Oh, who am I doing this work for? Oh yes, he likes it done this way'. It was done the HGH way!

Once this is done, your group might want to look at all the other things the business does and start to record all these into your systems manual. If you are an AVN member this will be 'System

Builder'. Building systems is a long haul. It is not an easy thing to do nor is it a quick fix. It does take time. I always say "Building systems will take you time. Systems built will save you time." One of the negative comments we used to get was that systems stifled creativity. I can easily understand why some might think that and I think it is wise to constantly tell yourself and your team that 'this is the way we do it until we find a better way of doing it and I want you all to be innovative and constantly look for and consider better ways'. When we do find a better way, that will be the new system!

HOW AVN CAN HELP

As an AVN Member you have access to the Michael Gerber DVD I referred to earlier. Show this to your team so that they gain a good understanding of why systems are important. All the roadmaps progressively build systems in to your practice. Roadmap 5 helps you establish a fully systemised business. The full suite of ready to tweak systems designed for an effective accountancy practice cover People, Leadership, Customer, Financial, Administrative, Operational and Marketing.

41 Involve Your Team In Building A Culture Of Lifetime Learning

If you thought the others were relatively easy to grapple with, you may find this one a little bit more difficult. It is a cultural thing all on its own. How do you develop in a business, a culture where people find it natural to seek out new learning? Where they want to read books or listen to CDs about improving their knowledge and skills in order to become more able to help clients/customers? Where they will read an article in a magazine or newspaper and see something relevant to a client. They will **want** to do these things because they recognise it as a natural thing to do. In fact, I would go even further and say that they won't even think about it. They will just do it!

It has become a habit. A great habit! It is part of the culture in your business!

This is not going to happen overnight. In fact, it will take as long as it takes and that will depend upon the existing culture in your business now.

So how are you going to achieve it?

I would suggest that you start by explaining to your team what you are trying to do. Tell them what you believe the benefits of such a 'culture' will be for them and also for the clients. Then through this group allow them to set up systems (liaising with the systems group), which will both encourage and measure the team's progress. You will need to incentivise them and agree targets with them. Allow them to have a budget for training in areas which are perhaps of a non-technical nature. We allowed each individual an annual budget to cover anything that they and the group felt fell within our definitions of lifetime learning. Our view was that anything which would naturally extend the talents of our team (and that of course included the business owners) and make them a more interesting and confident person, was totally acceptable. If they wanted to learn to play the piano, that was fine. If they wanted to learn to drive a car, then fine. If they wished to join a gym, provided they had set goals and they were to be measured, then that was also fine. We all had a responsibility to use the time and budget wisely and it was not there to be abused. This was a serious matter and as long as everyone was serious about it, then that was fine. In fact, it was better than fine (feeling inwardly negative everyday) it was fantastic.

We found that the initial volunteers for this group, and it was the smallest group, were ladies. What did that tell us? I am not sure but, they were a very dedicated group. After a few months the chairperson said she would like to take an NVQ in training and development. This was part of her lifetime learning programme. It was within her budget and highly relevant. She did complete the programme and she was very successful.

She asked if it would be appropriate for her, through the group, to carry out the role of the firm's Training Officer. This was a big bonus to one of our partners who got very frustrated with this task. He continued to be the 'official' Training Officer but he had effectively delegated much of the work to this young lady who then realised the amount of work that was involved. That in itself was a small triumph, as she told others and more people understood why it was such an important role.

The group also suggested that a rather untidy storeroom be converted to the HGH learning zone. A budget was agreed by the group in consultation with the 'policy advisers' in that group and the work was carried out. It genuinely inspired me to see people volunteering to help with moving old carpets and decorating this room. The furniture was ordered and the shelving installed. The technical library, which was scattered throughout the building was brought together and collated. A large pin board was placed upon the wall. People were encouraged to put anything that they thought might be of interest to others including of course, our clients, onto this board. Our team were encouraged to use the room in whichever way they felt benefited them. This usually meant having their lunch, listening to the radio, or watching the TV. But that was okay. They were in there developing the habit of contributing to the process of continuous learning.

HOW AVN CAN HELP
Helping your team adopt the mind-set around lifetime learning can be a challenge which some will embrace and some simply won't. Sometimes it's assumed that business related learning is dull and boring. The book I referred to earlier – 'Who Moved My Cheese' – is a great example of a business book that's not dull and boring because it's been created as a fun story that's entertaining but contains important learning points too.
Some prefer to read, some listen and others prefer to attend a physical event and get involved. At AVN we help with all three preferences.
In System Builder we have many great book recommendations

for people who prefer reading. There's a full library of audio recorded presentations covering every aspect of business improvement and this library is regularly added to. Every month we deliver live online training events that you can participate in with your entire team, perhaps in the conference room. After the presentation you have the opportunity to confer and share ideas and discuss next step actions based on the learning you've undertaken as a team. Of course, we run in-house workshops throughout the year and all team members are most welcome.

42 Have Non-Technical Team Meetings

Now I know there is the danger of having meetings for meetings sake. Some 'comic' put on our notice board the message 'Hold a meeting today – it's the practical alternative to work!' The truth was, at that time we were having meetings for meetings sake. We were not having meaningful meetings and nothing ever really changed as a result of having them.

What do I mean when I say 'non-technical meetings'? Well, I am not talking about updates on work in progress or what audits need to be planned or who in which department is going to look after which client! I am talking about bringing your team together to talk about things like:

- Understanding the vision of your business.
- Defining and agreeing the core purpose of the business.
- Defining and understanding the core values of the business.
- Carrying out a SWOT analysis on the business.
- Carrying out an all team happiness survey and studying the results.
- Perhaps discussing something that has come from the life time learning focus group.

These are only some examples. It is also important to use these meetings as an opportunity to train all the team in various areas of business knowledge. It could be things like:

- Understanding the relevance of defining your ideal customer.
- Why the 80/20 Pareto principle is so powerful.
- Or a whole choice of things, such as most of the topics covered in this small book.

If you are an AVN member you will have access to BBF (Business Builder Forum) within System Builder. All of these are powerful training tools when used with your team. These meetings are always a great opportunity to tell people what is going on and to get their valuable feedback.

Spend time on training your team and always have a 'celebration day'.

HOW AVN CAN HELP
As mentioned here, all of the BBF's are available in System Builder. These are the audio recorded presentations I've referred to. They cover all aspects of business and the library is regularly added to. For each of the exercises I've mentioned there is a resource in System Builder that will provide guidance on why and how to implement each of them.

43 Have Celebration Days

We had an annual celebration day. I said earlier that this took the place of one of the normal days for our focus group meetings. We had our celebration day in the summer, either June or July, simply because the weather allowed us to do more things. It worked liked this:

We would hire a hotel room close to us and meet up at around 9am. The partners would have worked out in advance (consulting the Managers and chairpersons from the focus groups) a presentation to give to everybody. The presentation was about what had happened over the last year; what had gone right and what had gone wrong. Our successes and our failure! What we had learnt, what we were going to do over the next year and where all of this fitted within our vision for the business. It was a simple, but powerful way of reminding us of the progress we were making and of re-stating our business goals. It revived our enthusiasm for the work and challenges ahead. It was quite inspiring to remember where we were this time last year. Sometimes when you think progress is slow you need to remind yourself just what you have achieved. These annual celebration days were a metaphorical photograph of the progress we were making.

After we had spent the morning looking at the 'past, present and the future' we would then have a fun event in the afternoon. The first time we went on a cruise on the river with a buffet lunch and bar provided. On another occasion we went to an outdoor adventure park. Another time the team went on a paintball shooting adventure. The point about all this was that we had fun and yet it was fun with a serious intent. Yes, costs were incurred. The hire of the room, the buffet, the bar and also the lost chargeable time on client work (we closed the offices), but it was a great investment which I believe brought massive rewards for the business and all of the team.

44 Have A One Page Plan

If you are an AVN member you will know what a 'OnePage Plan™' is. If you are not, then for your benefit briefly, it is a clever and simple (aren't the best things always simple) method of stating on a single sheet of A4 paper, what your business goals are, what your key drivers in your business are, what the KPIs are and what the ultimate measure of success is in your business. The unusual thing is that it starts from the bottom of the page and works its way up. It was the brainchild of the AVN chairman, Steve Pipe. In my opinion it is a much

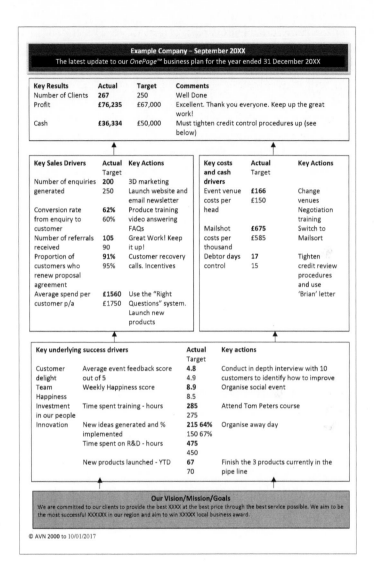

improved version of the Kaplan and Norton Balanced Scorecard. It is a great way of measuring successes and failures as it measures things that are important to your success which don't normally get included in any annual or monthly management accounts.

It's a fantastic tool to build your monthly reporting

management meeting around. It forms a major part of that agenda simply by working through the key measures and comparing actual with budget.

45 And Share It With Your Team

Why share this stuff with your team? In many businesses, the owners have a great reluctance to share information about the business with their employees. I can understand this. If you are very successful you might think that if you tell them, they will immediately want a pay rise. That might be so if you have engendered that sort of culture. The strange thing though is that most successful business do share this sort of information with their employees. Not necessarily what the profit is, but lots of the other things! I have done many team surveys now and one thing I do know is that most of them would like to know how the business is doing. Are we on target? Are we being successful? If they had this information most would use it appropriately. People generally want to help the business they work for become successful. Why? Well, because they feel good and it makes them proud to know they are working in a successful business. Maybe they will want rewarding, but why should that be a problem? If things are not going so well and you tell them so, they might be able to adapt and improve things to make it successful. People are generally far more motivated when they know what's going on. So tell them and use a 'one page plan'.

I often get asked how much should you tell your team and when should you start to tell them? If you have a current culture where nothing has previously been shared, don't suddenly start to give them all the details. This can scare people and may make them think the business is about to collapse! 'He's never told this before. What's going wrong?' Start by giving information that is helpful to them either in their department or themselves specifically. Any information which will enable them to perform to a higher level is helpful. Simply by having billing targets for people and the whole firm, is in itself very useful. Measuring those targets and reporting on actual and budgeted is a great start.

As time goes by you should consider giving more detailed information to your team. The culture in your organisation will be changing and such detail will no longer seem scary to your people. Eventually you will wonder why you didn't do it years ago. Trust people to use the information intelligently. They are not likely to let you down.

All this is part of the bigger picture. Time and time again you will read the word 'communication' in this book. This is part of that process and is essential to your business success.

HOW AVN CAN HELP
The Team Meeting agenda that I've previously mentioned includes going through the OnePage Plan™ with your team.

46 Have An Immaculate Place To Work

On my visits to around 350 accountancy businesses I have experienced all sorts of offices and facilities. I have to say that in the vast majority of cases the offices were well below the standard I would consider appropriate. Am I so fussy? I do not think so.

We spend around 40 plus years working in our office environment. Many work about 50 to 60 hours a week for about 46 weeks in those 40 plus years. That adds up to a whole load of hours. Most accountants I know, and all the people who work for them, have nice homes. Well decorated, warm, well furnished, clean and comfortable. Why would you want to work in conditions that are different to those you have at home? I don't know why, but I do know many who do seem to work in those conditions. What do your clients think? I can imagine they would generally prefer you to go and visit them. What do you employees think? I would imagine they would prefer to stay at home.

It was Michael Gerber who said something along these lines – "Your business should look as if it is the first day of business on each day of business!" He used Disney as his classic example. If you have ever been to Disneyland you will know the parks are immaculate! Every night certain bits get painted. Yes, every night! When I was there I saw young men with spatulas and paper cups cleaning gum off the streets. It's as fresh and inviting as the first day it opened. That's how your business should look!

47 Analyse Your Clients – To Death!

What do you know about your clients? Most accountants don't even know how many they have, let alone which one of them produces the most revenue. Even if they know which ones command the largest fee, they do not necessarily know whether they are generating a profit from them. The most successful businesses know all there is to know about their customers.

I referred earlier to the 'Pareto Principle'. Alfredo Pareto first made an observation whilst looking at the distribution of incomes in Italy in the 19th Century. The principle suggests that there is likely to be an 80:20 relationship somewhere in a set of data. It does not suggest that there will be. However, looking into the data and applying the principle is likely to produce some very interesting results. Simply asking which 20% of your customers produce 80% of your revenue will be enlightening. This is particularly so when you then look at the remaining 80% who are producing only 20% of your revenue. You may discover another interesting fact! 80% of your hassle comes from this 20% of revenue. You may then ask yourself 'Why am I working with these customers when they produce so little revenue and give me so much grief?'

When you have done that exercise, look and see if these larger customers are actually profitable customers. They may produce the revenue, but do they produce the profit? There is an expression, which I love and quote frequently, *"Turnover is vanity, profit is sanity, and cash is reality."* We often make the mistake of servicing the biggest customer first when actually they are the least profitable. You need to know who contributes what!

I know an accountancy business which knows exactly what each customer contributes to the profit of the business. They are constantly looking for ways to improve that profit. By taking this action they are, by definition, looking at ways to add value to the relationship with the customer. They are not simply increasing the fees. They are looking at ways to be more efficient and seeing how they can add real value to the relationship from which, as a result, the customer will want to pay higher fees.

Here are a few more questions which you might want to ask yourself about your customers. If you don't know the answers then perhaps you might need to find them out.
- Do you know what your customers buy from you?
- Do you know how often they buy from you?
- Do you know what their total spend (per annum) is?
- What do you think they might buy from you if you told them you were able to supply it?
- Where are they situated?

- Who do they know that you might like to have as customers?

This is by no means an exclusive list of questions. There are many more. The purpose of doing this is to demonstrate that the more detailed knowledge you have about your customers, the better the chances of you being successful. You might ask why this should be so. Well, if you know what they buy, it helps you sell other things. If you know how often they buy, it may help you sell to them more frequently. If you don't tell them about all the other things you can supply, they may never buy those things from you. Worse still, they may buy them from somebody else. If you know where they are situated it might show you have a cluster of your best clients in a certain locality. Would that assist you in gaining more of these types of clients in that locality? Perhaps!

HOW AVN CAN HELP

There's also an exercise you can use in System Builder which helps you to grade your clients. There are additional points to consider and the exercise gives you a clear picture of where your clients are situated on a grading scale. Jonathan explains more about grading clients later in this book.

48 Remember Profit Is A Consequence Of A Successful Business

When did you ever hear an entrepreneur say that their purpose for being in business was to make money? It disappoints me to hear that answer being given by so many business owners (and accountants). I would like to bet a million pounds to a penny that those who say that are likely to be the least successful ones. Many people do start a business because they are tired of working for somebody else and they feel they can do it better. So, they start a business and then find they are not actually running that business, but working for themselves. They just have another job. Now this may suit them very well and they carry on doing things this way and are happy as long as it keeps them in the standard of living to which they have become accustomed. I am not being critical of that because that is their choice.

However, if you want more than this, if you want to make a real difference and you are passionate about wanting to create a business, you must realise that your primary goal has to be to build a great business. A successful business, which as a result will be profitable! Profit is an outcome! It should not be the primary goal. It will happen naturally if you do all the other things correctly. So, concentrate on the great business, not the profit. The profits will follow!

49 Have Targets For Your Team

So many times I hear accountants say they are not as profitable as they would like to be. I think that as accountants we really need a paradigm shift! We are trained to think that if you run an accountancy business you should expect to make a profit within certain parameters of your turnover. Forty years ago it used to be 40% of your turnover. It then fell to about 30% and in our case, at its worst, our profit fell to around 22% of our turnover. I know accountants who are actually achieving around 50%. They are achieving these very high profit figures because they have moved away from the principle of cost plus pricing based upon hourly rates.

The dilemma for many though is they are currently so inefficient that to move from where they are now to the value pricing principle in one step is a step too far. In one go perhaps it is! I would recommend you need two or possibly three steps.

The first of these steps is to agree targets – for everyone.

Why have targets for yourself and your team? Well, we have all heard the expression 'What you can measure you can manage'. If you agree targets it will assist in managing the work through your business. Please note, I am not suggesting you set targets. I am suggesting you agree targets. There is an enormous difference. Imposing a target is likely to get you poorer results than agreeing them. If you explain to your team why you want to have targets and ask them to suggest theirs, there is a strong possibility they will set themselves a target in excess of the figure you were thinking of. People like to achieve. It is in our nature to want to do better than we did before. It's a natural competitive element in our psyche. You need to have systems which will allow you/them to measure how they are doing and a reporting process in place. You also need a reward system which recognises results! So how do you set about agreeing targets?

It is simple really. If you refer to the template opposite, you will see that for each individual you calculate the maximum possible hours each team member can possibly work, adding value to your clients. This really means the amount of billable hours they can work in a year. This process is really valuable because in carrying out this exercise you are identifying all the things people do that are non-billable. In doing that, you get everybody to focus on how they spend their time. Are they doing things only they need to do? Do I need to take as long as that or is there a quicker way? Remember everybody's calculation will be different. Most of your team will have certain responsibilities that are specific to them. They may perhaps have different training requirements. We assumed in our calculations that people would be sick during the year and we put in an allowance of two days! This may be an issue in your business or it may not. By acknowledging the fact, you are indicating that most people do not take any or much sickness and that can be a powerful message for those who unfortunately abuse your good nature!

If you go through the process of sitting with your team and identifying these non- billable areas you ultimately get to the point where they are agreeing that what's left is billable time. If you apply their charging rate, you then get a billable value for each team member. If you do this for everybody and add it all up, what do you get? Then compare this with you actual billing! Is there a difference? For most firms there is a big difference. They usually identify a surplus of what they are capable of billing compared to what they are actually billing. This is the black hole!

Template
Calculation of potential billing

An Example calculation
For a business operating with Focus Groups etc

Assuming a 36.25hour week.

Total working year is a possible   1885

Non-billable time:

Bank Holidays	8 days x 7.25hrs =	58.00
Annual holidays	20days x 7.25hrs =	145.00
C P D	5days x 7.25hrs =	29.00
AVN Training	4days x 7.25hrs =	36.25
Weekly non- chargeable	46 x .50 hrs =	23.00
Focus groups	10 x 1.50 hrs =	15.00
Celebration Day	1 x 7.25 hrs =	7.25
Focus group chairperson	10 x 1.00hrs =	10.00
Promotional Event	1 x 11.00hrs =	11.00
Specials (Identify – be specific)12 x 1.50hrs=		18.00
Loss committee	12sessions x 1.50hrs =	18.00
Sick	2 days x 7.25hrs =	14.50

Total non-chargeable time per annum   385

Potential billable time   1500 hrs

Assume normal charge rate is £ 50 per hour

Potential Billable value is   £75,000

This is the first step in actually identifying a problem and at the same time starting to solve it. You know:

- Your surplus capacity and...
- You have agreed targets with your team.

50 Agree Targets For You And Your Partners/Directors

How can you have targets for others if you don't set them for yourselves and your fellow business owners? You can't. It is as simple as that. Anyway, why would you not want to include yourselves in the same process? If you identify your own non- billable activities that helps you and others gain clarity about their roles in the business (see idea 13). Whether you like it or not, you are a substantial element of the revenue and therefore profit possibilities in your business. The ICAEW in the valuable report 'Building The Sustainable Practice' states that substantial evidence suggests the most profitable practices are those where the business owners have around 1000 hours of billable time. 1000 hours of adding value! I am not saying here that you must have that many hours of value, but it will greatly increase your profitability if you do or are approaching that figure. It may be that not all of you will achieve such a high level of billable hours, but in going through the process you will see who does what and also start to value the contributions of your fellow business owners. Or on the other hand it may bring to light some interesting facts! Sometimes some partners are spending a great deal of time in areas which are of very little value. If this is the case, you must tackle the issue head on.

51 The Zude (The Zone Of Uncomfortable Debate) Or Confronting The Brutal Truth

The problem with most partnerships is they don't like to discuss sensitive things. They do not like to upset one another. It is understandable. Not many people are confrontational, but sometimes it pays to be. Not in a deliberately provocative way, but in a way that gets to the heart of the problem. A way that gets the conversation into the areas where it is uncomfortable! This is not easy to do and it is sometimes best done by the non-executive Director. The nasty b****** you have hired to ask the awkward questions. Very often, if there is an issue, you may find it is shared by others, and nobody wants to say anything. You will probably find they want to deal with it, but they do not know how. Use great questions to steer the conversation to the area where you know there is a problem and stay there until you are satisfied all the issues have been dealt with.

Sometimes issues do not get resolved and that's when you know you have a choice. Is this something you can live with or is it so fundamental to the business and perhaps your own core values, meaning you cannot carry on unless something changes? If so, you must realise there are even bigger questions which need to be answered. Do not avoid the questions!

52 Value Price Wherever You Can

Many people think that because I am an advocate of job costing I do not believe in value pricing. This is far from the truth. As I said earlier, job costing (time sheets) should be a measure of internal efficiency and not the basis of value for billing.

There are many books written about 'Value Pricing' and some of the best are by Ron Baker. I am not going to go into the principles of why you should or how you should use value pricing. I am simply saying you should use it wherever and whenever you can. I remember all too well that before I became wise, I gave far too much away and I know many accountants who continue to do this. Even when they raise a bill they undervalue what they have delivered to their clients. We often think 'Oh, I cannot charge that much'. But how often do we even think about asking our clients to value it and pay to the value they think we have created or even saved them. I know many accountants who are now becoming wise and are extrapolating the savings to really demonstrate the benefit of what they have done for the client. And why not! The savings may not be for just one year, but many.

We used to do business planning for clients and we would ask them to value the day by giving them a guideline and asking them to price the day accordingly. We would tell them that if they did not value it, they should not pay anything or only pay to the value they thought they had received.

There are lots of opportunities to value price and you should be imaginative and trial some services. Some immediate ones that come to mind are:
- Incorporating a business.
- Tax planning strategies.
- Business planning days.

Even tax investigation work can be value priced, especially when you have a successful outcome.

I am not suggesting there is much scope when doing compliance work as clients will value it at the low end of the value equation. Compliance work is a commodity, but where you have delivered value to the client, recognise it. Explain the value to them and then attach the fee, perhaps by way of a percentage, extrapolating the savings over a number of years wherever you can.

As previously mentioned, pricing is one of the first areas AVN help you to develop and we supply software tools to help make the process of value pricing much simpler. The training we provide helps you understand the concepts of value pricing and price psychology. To complement the software we give you step by step processes to follow that are proven to significantly increase both your conversion rate and the fee you would normally quote.

53 Grade Your Clients

Why grade clients? Well, if you know how many good ones you have, it helps you get more good ones! If you know why you have poor clients, it might help you improve them to be good and even great ones!

I suggest you use a simple grading system. We used an A to E system and most importantly we did not allow the size of the fee to be part of our initial criteria. We graded the size of the fee on a 1 to 3 basis. This meant we could have some really great clients paying a big fee, i.e. an A1 client. We also had some great clients paying a very small fee, i.e. an A3 client. Conversely, we had some bad clients also paying big and small fees, although I have to say that the bad clients were more often paying very low fees.

We used the ICAEW's grading system and varied it according to our own circumstances. We decided to extend the criteria to include D and E clients. Our fee criteria was as follows:

- Fees over £5000 – 1.
- Fees over £1000 and up to £5000 – 2.
- Fees up to £1000 – 3.

Yours may be very different.

An example of this is shown on the following page.

CLIENT ASSESSMENT FORM

Client Name: .... Completed by: .... Date: ....

Fee Category	Range Used
1	Above £5000
2	Up to £5000
3	Up to £1000

Estimated Annual Fees: ....

Fee Category (1, 2 or 3): ....

Problem Areas   Yes   No

		Yes	No
1.	Usually late in bringing in records or responding to queries	☐	☐
2.	Always expects to "jump the queue"	☐	☐
3.	Significant bookkeeping or similar problems within the last two years	☐	☐
4.	Aggressive attitude to partners and/or staff	☐	☐
5.	Staff hate working on this job	☐	☐
6.	Usually ignores any advice given	☐	☐
7.	Dubious honesty or integrity	☐	☐
8.	Inland Revenue/VAT Investigation	☐	☐
9.	Recovery has fallen below 85 per cent in either of the last two years	☐	☐
10.	Disputed fees within the last two years	☐	☐
11.	Been in debt over 90 days within the last two years	☐	☐
12.	Never refers new clients	☐	☐

TOTAL   ☐   ☐

Category	No of No Answers
A	11 or 12
B	8, 9 or 10
C	7 or less

Problem category (A, B or C) ....

Overall category ....

Whichever system you use, it is a great idea to grade your clients. It is another way of finding out more about them and this enables you to manage them better and make more informed decisions. I would strongly suggest you remove the fee size from the initial grading though, as this may cloud your decision about a potentially great client.

54 Sack Some Clients

Why do we, as accountants, work for people who we do not like? Well, I can understand that perhaps we might if they are 'big' clients who pay on time, take our advice, and are appreciative of what we do. Having said that, if they did those things we would probably like them anyway!

No! I am talking about clients who never pay promptly, do not take our advice, are sometimes rude either to us or members of our team. They never seem to appreciate what we do, deliver things late, constantly whinge, and tell us when they have done something and want us to sort it out for free! We all have them and some of us still have. Why? Make a big decision that says, 'From today I am only going to work with people who do none of these things. Every time I get a new client who will **not** be a moaner or whinger, I am going to sack a client who is. If I am lucky enough to get a new client with a £5000 fee, I can afford to sack 10 clients with £500 fees and be actually a lot better off'.

In fact, ask your team which clients they would like to sack. I remember one firm I worked with had a policy of asking their team every month for the name of a client they would like to get rid of. The partners were brave in doing this and had to (unless they could give a very good reason why not) tell the client they no longer wished to act for them and would refer them to another firm in their locality. If they had a good reason, they had to convince their team why they would not sack the client. As with all these things, if you want to involve your team, you have to respond to their requests or give compelling reasons why you cannot in order for them to understand the decision. If you constantly ignore what you ask them, they lose faith in you and simple ask themselves, 'Why bother to ask us because you never listen to anything we say anyway?'

It is your business. Take control and stop working with nasty people!

HOW AVN CAN HELP
Type 'sacking' into the System Builder knowledge base and you will find a letter you could use to help with this process.

55 Have A TLC (Tender Loving Care) Package For Your Best Clients

When you have graded your clients and you know who your A1 clients are then start by having a 'TLC' programme for them. It does not have to be complicated. Ours was simple. We had a system whereby our A1 clients would get a non-technical telephone call from the partner or client manager at least once a month, simply to ask, 'How are you?' 'Is there anything you need any help with?' 'Can we help in any way?' it did not need to be a telephone call. If we were in their vicinity, we would call in to see them. Guess what? Around five to ten per cent of those calls would result in a request for additional work!

Even if it did not, as was the case on many occasions, at least they knew we cared about them.

HOW AVN CAN HELP
There is a great audio-recorded presentation on customer

service in System Builder called 'Crowning the Customer'. In addition, use OnTrack with every single client annually and more frequently with your best clients. OnTrack is a simple tool that helps you deliver more proactive help to your clients which wows them and improves their loyalty towards you. OnTrack enables you to do this in a high impact, low effort way.

56 Systematically Remind Them Of The Value Of The Relationship

Even if you provide a brilliant service to your clients you will always disappoint some. It is inevitable you will do this. After all, it is human nature and you cannot please everybody all the time.

The thing that really used to annoy me however, was when you knew you were doing a great job but the client always thought someone could do it better. It was a real disappointment to hear them say such things and if they then went to another accountant, I felt betrayed. I really used to think that. Now I realise that it was my fault! Yes, my fault! You see, I was guilty of not telling the client about what we had done and clearly explaining the value of the work we had delivered.

I know a firm of accountants who recognise this as a real danger. However, they have a system to deal with this. They simply tell the client every year (their A 1 clients) of the value they have helped create for that client. It can be tax savings through compliance work. It can be tax savings through tax planning. It can be value creation through business advisory work. The important thing is they are reminding their clients of the value of their relationship. They not only do it on an annual basis, but they accumulate the figures so that at any time in the relationship they can show the total value of it! Neat isn't it? So simple as well! This is a great process to use when you are negotiating the fixed fee for the following year. A time when you are most exposed to an attack from a competitor! Reminding your client of the value in the relationship allows them to make more of a connection with the fixed fee.

Why would anyone want to leave you when they can see how much you do for them and are able to compare it to the cost of your services?

HOW AVN CAN HELP
There are many resources to help. Type 'communicate value' into the System Builder knowledge base. The first place to start is an action resource called 'AR – Making the value of your work obvious'. There is also an effective pricing training resource – 'Effective Pricing Module 4 Workbook' which is worth having a read through for additional help.

57 Ask Them What They Think Of You

I started to ask my clients what they thought of us and it scared me silly to start to do this. I really was frightened to ask them just in case they gave me an answer which I did not want to hear. I would simply ask them "Is everything okay? Is there anything we could do better?" Of course, I was only brave enough to start this process with the clients I thought would give me a favourable answer and they usually did. When I realised that asking such questions took you into a different area of conversation I knew that it was even more important to put the same questions to the clients I was less sure about. I got some very interesting answers. It usually took me to a new level of awareness about myself and the business. The clients were generally flattered to be asked and it helped to improve relationships and also helped in the process of them valuing what we did. It also helped us improve in areas where we were not so good! And that's got to be of value – to everyone!

58 Ask Them For Testimonials

So, you ask them "How are we doing?" and they tell you. If you like what you hear, why not ask them another question? Ask them for a written testimonial. Many clients will happily give you one and it is a really simple, yet powerful marketing tool to use in your business. Many will probably say, "What do you want me to say?" I used to say "Shall I write it for you? I can then email it to you and if you are happy with it then you can produce it onto your letter headed paper and send it to us in the stamped address envelope I can give you." They sometimes amended the letter, but that was never a problem. The thing was, it made it easy for them to say "yes" to giving us a testimonial.

59 Ask Them For Three Referrals

Now you know they are willing to give you a testimonial and believe me, if you are doing it right then many will, why not ask them the next question, which is simply, "Who else do you know who would benefit from working with us in the same way we work together?" In fact, the knack is to ask not for one referral, but to ask for three. If you ask for one you may be lucky and get one, but more often than not you will be told that they are not sure they know anyone. If you ask for three you might get the response "Oh, I'm not sure I know three, but I think I can give you one!"

Great result!

> **HOW AVN CAN HELP**
> Type 'referrals' into the System Builder knowledge base. This will reveal many results which provide alternative approaches to getting referrals from your clients and also from other people you may come in to contact with.

60 Remember Your Clients Know More People Just Like Themselves

Always remember to ask the right people though. If you have graded your clients, you would start with your A1 clients and not your E3s. People usually know and socialise with people very much like themselves. It sounds obvious doesn't it, and it is, but it is very often forgotten. If you want more A1s then ask your existing A1s.

61 Recruit Only The Best People

How often have you made a bad recruitment decision? I know I did many times. The trouble was we needed someone and we needed them now, so in the end we would recruit anyone! They always turned out to be bad recruitment decisions. Learn to say no! Never recruit just because you need to and there is no one else around. Wait and be patient and of course, if you plan well ahead this situation may never occur.

HOW AVN CAN HELP
Type 'recruit' into the System Builder knowledge base – there are two documents which can help with recruiting – 'AR - Advertising for new team and clients,' and 'Ways of Recruiting New Team Members'.

62 Recruit For Attitude And Not Just Skill

Now I am not sure everyone would agree with me here, but I firmly think that the person with the correct attitude and the capability to learn a skill is a far better recruitment bet than someone with the wrong attitude and with all the skills in the world. Some also say that in today's world it is harder than ever to find people with the correct attitude. I sometimes think that it is because nobody has ever explained to them what the correct attitude is and this may be true.

I like the story of the young sales assistant who never displayed the correct attitude and was always being complained about by the floor manager. In the end the floor manager reported him to the store manager. The store manager asked to see the young sales person and explained the problem to him. The young man said "But what do you mean by the correct attitude?" That was an interesting reply, don't you think? When the store manager explained, the young man then went about his business with a smile and a willingness never previously shown before. Now I am not sure this is a true story, but I think you get the point. Some people do need to have things we take for granted explained to them and when they understand, they may then change their behaviour.

I do believe that the right attitude is all important in a service related business.

63 Involve Your Team In The Recruitment Process

We learnt that it was a useful technique to have your team involved in the recruitment process. We, as partners, would allocate the initial interview to the 'team partner' and if he/she thought them good enough, they would be interviewed by a small number of the senior team. They would also have the opportunity to take the potential new team member around the offices and introduce them to the rest of the team. This gave them an opportunity to meet and evaluate the new team member and for them to decide whether they 'felt comfortable' with them. It also gave the potential new employee a chance to meet the team and see if they felt right with them. If all was going well some, or all of the partners, would have a final interview with the potential employee to see if everything was fitting as it should. This way we usually found far more suitable people who we knew would fit into our new and developing culture.

HOW AVN CAN HELP
Talk to your Practice Growth Expert to learn more about the AVN recruitment process as they are very much involved in the recruitment process. AVN's recruitment process often appears a little over the top to some, but in reality it's far less time consuming and less expensive than employing the wrong

people. It's not infallible, but it significantly improves the chances of finding a person whose values and beliefs are a closer match to yours and your team culture and who buys in to your vision.

64 Have An Agreed 'Internal Core Values' Statement

I learnt this simple and powerful process from a client. I was delivering 'BoardView' – the AVN package of acting as a non-executive director. During one of those director meetings, the Managing Director referred to their core values statement. I asked what this was and of course he told me and produced a copy of it for my reference. It was such a good idea that I went back to our office and set about developing our own. In one of our team meetings I asked all of us to consider the way we would like to be treated internally in the business. We captured the ideas onto a flip chart and from this we developed our own internal core values statement.

Some of our team thought it strange to ask ourselves such a question and then feel the need to capture it on paper! They thought it unnecessary. These are natural values, aren't they? Why do you need to write them down? However, when we explained that it was sometimes a good thing to have a written code of behaviour and to be able to refer to it when necessary, they reconsidered. Some things are thought to be 'givens', but that does not always mean we practice them. They became part of our management tools as we were able to refer to them when there was an issue between certain team members. We could refer them to our core values and that helped resolve the dispute.

The internal values statement was also used when recruiting new team members. They were asked to read it and to comment upon it. It was a useful way of assessing their thoughts and ideas on the subject and also many said it was 'different'. Their existing employers did not have anything like it. It was a differentiator and for some the reason why they wanted to join us rather than our competitors. It also gave us an indication as to their attitudes about such things and a clue as to whether they would fit in with us and our culture.

HOW AVN CAN HELP
An example of this is in System Builder called 'Team Commitment'.
During AVN Roadmap 2 we help you discover your values as part of a workshop day. This is an exercise you can take back and also apply with your team.

65 Have An Agreed 'External Core Values' Statement

Having sorted our core values for ourselves internally, it seemed relevant to sort them for our customers and indeed any other stakeholders we considered we had. We had to ask ourselves how we wanted to treat and be treated by these outside parties. The usual things were mentioned, courtesy, politeness etc. Others like 'we wanted to be paid on time, valued and consulted' were also high on the list. We used this 'values statement' when talking to potential clients to gauge their reaction. If they responded positively, this gave us an indication as to how they might behave when and if we started to work with them. Obviously, this worked both ways. We also recognised that they wanted to be treated appropriately and the values statement also included how we would behave with them. Simple stuff! Obvious stuff! Common sense not commonly used.

66 As Business Owners Do A SWOT (Strengths, Weaknesses, Opportunities And Threats) On Your Business

I know we have all heard about the famous SWOT analysis. It seemed it was once thought of as a really simple, yet powerful diagnostic tool to use on a business. It seemed to go out of fashion but has now made an amazing resurgence. It is a great exercise to be carried out by the business owners, but as will be pointed out later, that is just the start. It is important to understand what the business owners think. But that is the point! It is only a start!

HOW AVN CAN HELP
Type 'swot' in to System Builder to get access to the template. The template contains incredibly helpful thought provoking questions against each section which will help when conducting the exercise.

67 Get Your Team To Do A SWOT On The Business

After the business owners, comes the team. They are likely to have a very different perspective on the SWOT than the business owners. It does not mean it is right, but is certainly cannot be wrong! What they perceive as a strength may well be and what they perceive a weakness probably will be. The chances are what they think is an opportunity could be and what they see as a threat probably will be. All the information gained from doing this exercise with the business owners and the team is highly relevant, important stuff to be used by the business owners to take the business forward. However good it is though, it will not be as important as doing a SWOT with the clients and perhaps some of your introducers and other professional connections.

68 Get Some Of Your Clients And Introducers To Do A SWOT On Your Business

This is where the real gems lie! Whatever you or your team think about your business, and as valuable as that is, it is not as valuable as what your clients or other professional connections think. They have a real handle on this because they see you from a completely different perspective. You need to understand what they think of you and how they perceive you. You may think it is incorrect, but how can it be when **they** think it!

The best way to run these events is to have one of your managers, or possibly two, (someone who has the confidence and personality) to act as a facilitator. Get say, six to eight of your best clients and say two of your 'introducers' into a comfortable room. Ply them with tea and coffee and use a flip chart to capture the comments. Explain that you will have a chance to meet with them afterwards for a glass of wine and a light buffet. Make it an event worth having. This in itself makes it a valuable marketing event and one that those taking part will remember. They will also be flattered you have asked them for their opinion. People loved to be asked for their opinion.

I have worked with a number of firms which have carried out a SWOT with clients etc. They have all said that the results were brilliant. It told them so much about their business that the whole process was invaluable. Their clients loved it as well. It also became a great opportunity to say to those clients "Would you like us to run one for you on your business, using some of your best customers?"

The Business Edge Programme   SWOT worksheet

STRENGTHS

What makes people buy from us?

What makes people recommend us?

What skills do we have and what are we especially good at?

What can we do that nobody else can?

What successes have we had recently, and why?

WEAKNESSES

What skills do we lack and what aren't we good at?

What do others do better than us?

What failures have we had recently, and why?

Why do people chose our competitors instead of us?

Why do previously happy customers leave us?

OPPORTUNITIES

What new products/services could we offer?

What new skills and capabilities could we acquire?

How could we become unique?

What new types of customers/markets/needs could we serve?

What changes in the market could we exploit?

What new ideas, techniques & technology could we use?

THREATS

What new ideas, techniques & technology could undermine us?

What are our competitors doing that could damage us?

Are there any legal, economic or political threats to us?

Are our customers' needs changing?

What other changes in the market could damage us?

Are there any other black clouds on the horizon?

What a great opportunity for an additional and valuable new service for your clients!

The previous page shows an example of the AVN SWOT analysis.

HOW AVN CAN HELP
Type 'Customer Forum' into the System Builder knowledge base and you will find 'AR - Customer forum and questionnaire' which can be used to run exactly the process Jonathan describes.

69 Remember The Best Client You Have Got Is The One You've Got Now

That is assuming they are clients that you are not considering sacking!

There are various statistics which suggest it is far more expensive to get a new customer than it is to look after an existing one. I am not sure which one is correct or even if that matters. It seems to me though that it is folly to keep on looking for new ones when you are losing them because you do not look after them. So, it is sensible to take the view that your existing customers are more important than looking for new ones. Remember that and look after your customers accordingly. Using the TLC package referred to earlier will help your retention and client loyalty, but putting the basics in place, like delivering your services on time, are vital.

There is very little point in trying to deliver new and innovative services to clients if you are not getting the basics right. Get the simple stuff right before moving onto the complicated.

70 But Also Remember The Most Important Client You Have Got Is Your Own Business.

Yes, I know you may think I am contradicting myself but I do use the words 'best' and 'important' appropriately. Far too often we spend too little time on our own business. We rush around looking after everybody else's business and ignore our own. I know we need to give our customers a great service. That goes without saying, but we also need to look after our own business. We need to allow ourselves (and others in our business) time to work on it! If you were to analyse how you spend your time between your business and your clients, I am guessing that your clients would win out every time. I am only suggesting you need to have more of a balance and to spend more of that time ON your business. There is a great exercise that you can carry out which will help you understand the imbalance that you possibly have.

Are you doing the right things as a business?			
Key areas the management team in your business is spending its time on	% of their time you wish they were spending on this area of the business	% of their time they are actually spending on this area of the business	Gap
Working IN the business on inward facing activities eg • Business management • People management • Administration • Other ways of working IN the inward facing parts of the business			
Working IN the business on customer facing activities eg • Winning new customers • Serving existing customers • Other ways of working IN the customer facing parts of the business			
Working ON the business to develop • Winning strategies for your firm • Better ways of serving/ helping customers • The skills and knowledge of your team • Other ways of working ON the business			
	100%	100%	

Notes *Does the gap analysis suggest you need to make changes in order to achieve your goals? If it does, what changes are you going to make?*

Do this exercise. It will help you make the changes. However, those changes may not happen unless you make them happen by blocking out some time!

71 Block Out Some Time

Most of us have a diary system. It is an essential tool in making sure we remember the things we are supposed to do and the places we are supposed to be. However, how many of us ever book an appointment with ourselves or our business. There may be the odd partner meeting or even a team meeting, but how much of our time is blocked out so we have the time to do some of the important stuff rather than just the urgent things?

If you have a manual diary I suggest you get a big **red** marker pen and block out lumps of time in your diary for you and your business. Decide which day of the week you want it to be and **do it**! If someone else controls your diary, get that person to do it and tell them that it must not be altered.

I remember working with a sole practitioner whose secretary looked after his diary. He told me that people were always altering it and he never seemed to get the time to do the things he had promised himself he would do on the Friday he had allocated to work on his business. I suggested to him he must inform all his team that this day was important. So much so that if anyone altered it, they would get a verbal warning. If they persisted in changing things they would get a written warning. If they still carried on, they would be dismissed! Whether he could or even wanted to do this, is not the point. It demonstrated to everyone that this was important and they must realise the seriousness of why his time was being allocated to his business.

HOW AVN CAN HELP
A tip from AVN – always block out time in the morning rather than the afternoon as you will likely get distracted by 'work' and find the afternoon drifts away. If you allocate the morning to work on your business, do this before you open your emails.

72 Have Great Reward Systems For Your Team

And I am not just meaning lots of salary. Money is, of course, very important in rewarding those who do a great job for the business, but there are other ways to reward your team.

My son-in-law once worked for a recruitment firm. He told me that the weekly prize for the best performer was a case of beer. It cost around £10 from the local supermarket, but he said the competition for the beer was immense. Not a lot of cost for a great week's performance. I am not suggesting you use this reward system, but you can see there are different ways to reward you team and you need to find one which really excites them. It may be time off. It may be a salary bonus. It may be a voucher for a well-known store. It may be extra holiday days. It can be many things, but make it different and exciting for them. Ask what they would like to have in the reward system and keep it under constant review.

Whilst we are talking about reward systems, I would like to mention another common failing we have. We certainly did. Isn't it sad when one of your team comes to see you and say that she/he has with regret decided to move to another firm? They don't want to, but the salary package they are offering is too good to miss. You have a hasty meeting with your partners, if you have them, or a hasty meeting with yourself, and come to the conclusion they are too good to lose so you offer them a better deal than the one they have currently been offered. They may decide to stay or they may, and you could not blame them, decide to move on because they feel they deserved that package without having to force your arm. And, of course, they are correct. Frankly you deserve to lose them. Why wait until you are forced to offer the right salary package to any one of your team. If you value them, pay them what they deserve and do it without them asking for an increase or telling you they have been offered a better package somewhere else.

73 Give Feedback To Your Team

I have spoken to many team members of accountancy businesses. The biggest complaint from them is that nobody tells them how they are doing. "We never get any feedback," is what they usually say. "I don't know how I am doing. Nobody tells me anything!"

People like to know how they are performing, even if it is not as good as it should be. They want to know what they may be doing wrong so that they can then do it right! Having a six-monthly appraisal is great, but you do need to give ongoing feedback on a day to day or an assignment by assignment basis. Having a constructive critique about how you are performing is so valuable for both parties. This is how we all learn to do things better and to repeat the things we are doing well. It also makes people feel valued and that is critical. It is just another significant element of how to have great communications with your team.

74 Listen To Your Team – Hear And Understand

We ask people for their opinion and what do we do
with it? Not much usually. Why? Well, I think there's a number
of reasons for this. We may not like what we hear or we may
simply not hear it in the first place. I used to say that I had an
open door policy. I did, in as much as my door was open unless I
was with a client. However, if someone asked to have a quick
word, I rarely asked them to come in and sit down. I would ask
them what they wanted and then would carry on doing
whatever I was doing. I may have been collecting some papers
together or finishing off a letter. I was not actually there for
them, hearing what they had to say. I thought I was, but that
person knew I was not paying them the attention they deserved.
I was actually being quite discourteous. We had spent many
hours endeavouring to get our team to open up and trust us so
that they would share ideas, and as soon as they did we did not
listen at all well and did not properly hear what they were
saying.

The management training skills course delivered to us in our
offices made us realise we were not as good at listening as we
thought.

then. AVN members have access to a piece of software called TeamMatters. Amongst other things TeamMatters often checks in with your team members and reports to you immediately via text or email to inform you if you need to deal with a problem a team member has before it begins to fester. Something that inevitably happens when people put off dealing with Team Matters.

75 Tell The Truth – To Everybody

Perhaps this seems like an obvious thing to do. It is! However, do we always do it? Unfortunately, this is not always so.

I am sure we would never be untruthful with a client, but we may couch what we have to say with words which make the facts a little more palatable. Does this change the content of what we are saying? Maybe! We do not want to upset anyone, least of all a valuable client because if we do they may not like us and if they do not like us perhaps they will go to someone else they may like. Someone who will tell them what they want to hear.

If we are not honest with them, eventually they will leave us anyway.

We need to be honest with everybody and that includes our clients, our team and importantly, ourselves. There are ways of saying everything, but the overriding message must be truthful and factual no matter how difficult it is to deliver. The art of great communication is to say it as it is, but in a manner which everyone accepts because they see the benefits of hearing it that way!

76   Mean What You Say

Sometimes we bite the bullet and say what needs to be said, but then we need to take some action to deliver on what we have said. This is when things get a bit tricky. It may have been difficult to say it, but it is going to be even more difficult to do something about it. So, what might we do? Nothing! Then the person we have the conversation with simply does not believe what we have said and even more importantly, does not believe whatever we may say in the future. If you say it, mean it and do something about it. Otherwise do not say it all.

77   Measure Your Under-Recoveries

I know that fixed price agreements based on value pricing are the right things to have, but you still need to measure whether the price you agreed is the correct price. You need to calculate whether you are being profitable with the price you quoted. Use the usual methods to do this, relating it back to the practice of having agreed targets for all your team and yourself. You will have records of time costs etc. Use these to measure your teams and your own performances and calculate whether the job is profitable.

If it is, how can you make it more profitable? If it is not, what are you going to do to make it profitable?

78 Identify The Reason For Your Losses And Take The Relevant Action

The reasons you lose on so many customers is down to many factors. You need to ascertain what those factors are and take action to make sure they do not arise again.

Some of those factors are listed below and some you will say are obvious. Yes, they are, but why not do something about them because they are not complicated.

- The fee is too low.
- We did work for them which was not within the scope of the fixed price agreed and we have not billed them.
- The wrong person did the work and they are too experienced and cost too much or an under qualified person did the work without the required experience.
- The work was poorly planned.
- We did not receive all the information in a timely manner and we had to keep picking up the file and put it down again. This always adds cost to the work.

The thing is, what do you do about it? Ignore it and carry on as before and repeat the errors next year or next month? Or do we do something/take action to make sure it does not happen again? The thing is that most of the reasons are repeated job after job. When you learn one thing, you can apply it repeatedly on many other customers. When you know what has gone wrong, devise a specific action to correct it and make someone accountable to take that action. One of the ways to ensure you take action is by having a Loss Committee.

HOW AVN CAN HELP
Using 'times up' and 'extra work orders' along with the systems for preparing accounts can help with many of these areas.

79 The Loss Committee

This is an idea we received from Graham Lamont and I think it is brilliant. We all know that when you make a loss on a client it is difficult to apportion blame or always understand why you have messed up. Why would we, as business owners, always know why?

The answer is that we probably don't. However, your team probably does. Graham suggested that we have what he referred to as a Loss Committee. Have three or four of your best people on the committee together with a partner. You meet once a month on a fixed day (because this is a system) and you go through all the losses on the previous months' billing. If it is one of your clients and you are on the committee, another partner would sit in instead of you and act as chairperson.

When we started this process it would have taken us all day to go through our losses, so to start with we just went through which were more than 10% of the fee. This still took a long time, but you need to endeavour to have the meeting last no more than an hour to an hour and a half.

We discussed why we believed a loss had occurred. What had gone wrong? Why did we make a loss and most importantly what would we do to ensure it did not occur again? We sometimes got the person who had carried out the work to come in and give what they thought was an explanation as to why it had occurred. Very often the reasons were those referred to in the previous idea. The big point though was that we decided what action we needed to take and most importantly – who was to take it.

Gradually as things improved the meeting got shorter and we looked at smaller losses, until nearly all the problems had been addressed and we not incurring such losses. Our recovery went from around 78% to over 95%. Not perfect! But a lot, lot better!

80 Have Great Credit Control

In a perfect accountancy business there would never be a need to have credit control. You would always be paid either in advance or by direct debit, thereby eliminating the need to have to chase any debt. However, it will take you some time to create that perfect business, so in the meantime you will need some credit control. So, who is going to do it?

I believe and some others do too, that the worst person to chase and look after debtors is you! It is very difficult to ask someone who you have good relationship with, for money. You will be full of good intentions. You will have that meeting with the client and on your agenda will be – 'I am going to ask him about the arrears and I am going to suggest a way of handling it'. No, you won't. You will get to the point where you intended to bring it up and you will suddenly feel that it is a bit difficult at the moment. The meeting has gone so well. I don't want to spoil it so I will deal with it the next time. There will be plenty of occasions similar to this or others like it. You are not the person to handle these issues. Get someone else.

Preferably a lady! If you think this a bit politically incorrect, well, sorry but it is true. Most women are more positive and less embarrassed about asking your clients for money. Many if not most, because it is statistically correct, of your clients will be male. Men find it much harder to refuse when being asked by a lady. A person other than you can be far more dispassionate about such matters. It is not their money they are asking for. They are more business-like and they know it is fair.

The other big advantage about having someone else do it for you is that it does not spoil the relationship you have with your customer. If they should complain to you, it is right and proper to point out to them the terms and conditions they signed up to when they became a customer. That is assuming of course you have these in place when you get a new one.

If they still do not like the way things are, then are they the right person to be working with? Probably not!

HOW AVN CAN HELP
There are many useful letter/email templates and strategies in System Builder which will help your team deal with credit control.

81 Constantly Test Your Pricing

I am not an expert in pricing. For that you need to perhaps speak to someone like Mark Wickersham of AVN. Mark has run many courses and written many books on this subject.

Some of the simple things I have learnt from Mark and others are:

- Your pricing methodology says a lot about you and your business brand. It goes back to the cheap and cheerful or expensive and exclusive image you want to create. Which is it to be?
- Never give an estimate. If you say, 'It is going to be between £1200 and £1500,' the customers thinks it will be £1200 and you are thinking £1500. Immediately there is a reason for a dispute. So always be precise and stick to it unless...
- You discover the work you are carrying out is different to what you originally quoted for. You need to immediately inform your customer and agree a revised figure given the additional work to be undertaken. Do this before you do any other work. Some of us just carry on believing that the customer will agree to an extra fee. Some will, but some will not.
- Some of us are better at negotiating a fee than others. If you find it difficult, perhaps let someone else do it. If you are literally a sole owner and have no one else to do this, perhaps consider going onto a course (maybe Mark Wickersham's) and get yourself more confidence.

- I remember early on in my membership of AVN Mark Wickersham talking about 'top down pricing.' He referred to someone going into a tailor's shop and wanting to buy a suit. I don't think many of us do that now, but the principle still applies. Unless you state the price range to begin with, the assistant is likely to show you the most expensive suits. You will probably say that it is too expensive and he will then show you another one at a lower price. You may buy it or you may again say that it is too expensive so he shows you a cheaper one again. I think you get the message. The chances are you will pay more for your suit than you originally thought. If he started at the bottom you would have paid less!

- Some of the aspects of pricing are quite scientific. I will leave that to the experts, but I do believe there is the perfect price. However, the challenge is to find it. You may know that airlines change the prices of their tickets millions of times before the flight ever leaves the ground. That is only one example of a complicated pricing procedure. Our profession does not work like that, but we do need to consider testing our pricing all the time. Sometimes we are too cheap and sometimes we may quote too much. The thing is, we need to find the right balance between the two. You know it is very frustrating when you give a quote and the response is – "Oh, that seems very reasonable." You know you have left something on the table. So constantly test your pricing.

The best way to price though and have no room for misunderstanding is to use a Fixed Price Agreement.

HOW AVN CAN HELP
At AVN we provide extensive training and provide many additional resources and 'how to' videos on pricing. With so many accountants competing on price it's important to move out of the competitive pricing arena and into the value pricing one. It's important to test prices and meeting price resistance is important. If you're not meeting price resistance when you're selling the value, you're not charging enough.
One of the pricing tools that AVN provides access to its

82 Use Fixed Pricing Agreements

I can't really believe that I have left this one for so long in this short book before getting to it! Frankly it is the one simple business idea that can make a massive difference to your business and the relationship you have with your customers.

You may recall in an earlier idea, I said you should never give an estimate. It will always be seen differently by you who gave it and the customer who heard it. What they heard will always be a lower amount. Be precise.

And the only way you can be precise is to give a fixed price and get it agreed in writing. You and the both bound by it. It provides many advantages:

- There can be no misunderstanding as to what is agreed.
- The precise nature of the scope of the work is in writing and is understood.
- If extra work is needed it can be clarified and the additional fee agreed.
- There are no nasty surprises for your customer. They know what to expect and so do you.
- When things are agreed in advance there can be no questioning after the work is complete.
- Because it is clear and precise it allows you to agree a payment in advance or at least payment by Direct Debit.

HOW AVN CAN HELP

Time's Up! – AVN's pricing software – automatically generates in depth Fixed Price Agreements and details the value your client can expect to receive for the fee. The Fixed Price Agreement is fully customisable and serves as a great starting

83 Get Paid In Advance (Or At Least By Direct Debit)

Obviously this follows on from the previous idea. The idea of getting paid in advance was up to only a few years ago, an absurd thought. How can we as an accountancy 'practice' ask for money in advance of us carrying out the work? There are now many firms who do and their clients are happy with this. Obviously if you do this, you certainly have to deliver the goods and give a great service, but is that not what you are striving to do anyway? For many of us though, I expect that this may be a step too far. However, getting paid by instalments should not be. Many firms do now expect their clients to pay by Direct Debit. It used to be by Standing Order before smaller businesses could get onto a DD system. The point is that getting your customer to agree to pay on a monthly basis should be the norm for all new customers.

I know many of the firms I have worked with have issues with this and I understand why. If you have businesses you have worked with for many years and they pay very quickly after you bill them, why would you ask them to pay by monthly DD? Perhaps you would not, but that is provided you bill them promptly and regularly.

However, there will be some of your existing customers who will be happy to be on DD and some of them may even prefer it. Never presume who would and who would not. Ask them all and explain the benefits for both their business and your own. Some of my older customers actually preferred it, because it helped their own cash flow (as well as mine).

By default, Time's Up! divides the fee to the customer over as many months as you would like, and allows you to select direct debit as a form of payment. AVN can help you to set up direct debits in your practice if you haven't already done so. During our training sessions, we provide scripts and insights in to how to encourage a client who's accustomed to paying in arrears, to paying in advance.

84 Stop Giving Stuff Away

I used to give loads of value away for free! A client would ring and ask a question like "How much Capital Gains Tax will I pay if I sell that flat I currently let out?" You know the kind of question you get asked. I would then do some mental calculations, ask a few questions and then give an estimate of the tax to pay. The client would then say, "Thanks for that," and then the conversation might end and the phone would go down. I would then put three units (15 minutes) down in my diary or however long it had taken, which meant at my charging rate, I had massively undervalued the information I had given to my client.

What I should have done was say something like this: "Fred, I am not sure at the moment and I will have to do a little research and some calculations. It may take me a little time. I will have to charge you £xxx and I can get back to you tomorrow with the information. That is okay with you, isn't it?"

Now I know that some of you are probably thinking that it is a bit immoral to charge say £200 for something that you can do in 15 minutes. Ask yourself this. Why can I do such a calculation in 15 minutes and my client cannot? The answer is simple. You have acquired skills and knowledge over a long period which your client does not have. Do you think that your client would give stuff away? If you do, perhaps you need to talk to him/her and get them to realise just what they are doing. There is also the possibility that Fred may say "Oh, that seems a lot. Perhaps I will leave it at the moment." Is that such a bad thing? If nothing else, you may have saved yourself some time and Fred now realises that your knowledge and skills cost money. They will value you more!

I also realise that you do not want to deter Fred from contacting you, but he does need to value your advice and this is all about getting the balance right. Too many times it is in your clients favour and anyway, you should be contacting him/her by being proactive (see no. 92). You can afford to be proactive when you charge the correct fee and stop giving stuff away.

HOW AVN CAN HELP
Time's Up! enables you to quote for one-off extra work orders that you, or your team, can use in order to provide a value based fee in advance and very quickly to your clients when they make those kinds of requests.

85 Don't Undervalue Yourself Or Your Team

We have talked about undervaluing yourself. But what about your team? I learnt from one of my best people that on occasions I did undervalue him and it made him quite cross when I did. Initially he would not say anything, but as we changed the culture in the business to one of a more open one he told me. It happened at the same time we were involving our team on why we made under recoveries on some work and David, (that was his name), said we were not charging the client enough. He simply told me that he felt, and others did too, a bit annoyed that when a lot of effort had gone into a customer's work, we the partners, were writing off a lot of the value created by the team. We were undervaluing it. David told me it was very demoralising for him and others. He told me that they felt very strongly about it. He even suggested that he or other members of the team should be responsible for billing the work they had done. They would explain to the customer the value of the work that had been undertaken if we did not have the courage to do so.

A great big lesson! Do not undervalue the work your team does as it can be a very significant negative factor.

86 Learn How To Say No!

Sometimes your success can be determined by what you do not do rather than what you do! Keeping your focus and concentrating on what is important (not always urgent) can be critical to your success. Therefore, learning to say no, can have a massive benefit for you and your business. It's so easy to say "yes." We like to say "yes" because we like to please people. We do not like to let them down so we say "yes," but far too often that creates problems for us and our business. We over commit to doing things and as a result we fail to do the things that are really important.

So remember, sometimes you need to say no, even if that means turning work away, enabling you to concentrate on doing the right things in your business. The important things in your business!

87 Learn To Accept A Silence

Silence is unusual! Silence can be embarrassing! We usually want to jump in and fill the hole created by silence. When I started to understand the power of asking great questions, I would steal myself to ask one. I got the inevitable silence. In my ignorance, I wanted to avoid this embarrassing silence and would jump in with another question or I would make a comment, worried that my client thought I had asked a silly question. It was only later when I had more confidence that I realised my client was thinking of the answer! In fact, I remember him saying so. He said to me, "Wait a moment Jonathan, I was thinking of the answer!"

I learned from Andy Gilbert that silence can be massively powerful. He told me that he once asked someone he was coaching a powerful question and waited for the answer. He got one and he said nothing. There was silence and then he got another answer. Silence! He got another answer and there was more silence. He waited for the sixth answer before he felt it was right to say anything. He then told me that the sixth answer turned out to be the most important of all and that if he had jumped in and stopped the process, the answer would never have been discovered and would have been lost.

Why do we find silence difficult? Why are we so reluctant to have silence?

88 Surround Yourself With Experts

Some people are frightened of people who know more than they do. Why? We cannot know it all. It would be impossible and if we did know it all, that would mean that we would have to do it all! That would mean that we would not get it all done.

A client of mine who was passionate about his business told me he wanted the best people. He wanted them working with him. He wanted them to share in his passion, but to be experts in their fields so that he did not have to worry about the right things getting done. He was, of course, right. Surround yourself with experts.

HOW AVN CAN HELP

The AVN accountability groups consist of your peers and an AVN Practice Growth Expert. You're able to tap into the brains of many others who will be stronger in some areas than you are and collectively provide great insights covering all areas of effectively running an accounting firm as a successful business. Our AVN Practice Growth Expert complements this great environment by bringing their own experience and knowledge to the group including 100% AVN resource knowledge and in addition, brings experiences and stories from other accountants in different groups.

89 Study And Learn From Other Great Businesses

There are so many things we can replicate in our business that other great businesses do. Just because we happen to be in the business of accountancy, does not mean that we cannot learn from other commercial activities.

Ask yourself a simple question:

- What other business have impressed you with what they do and how they do it?

Likewise ask yourself the opposite question:

- What other businesses have really cheesed you off by what they do and how they do it?

What lessons can you learn from the answers to these questions and how might you incorporate those answers into your business? Start to do the great things that really pleased you and make sure you are not doing the things which cheesed you off.

HOW AVN CAN HELP

The criterion for AVNExcellence and indeed the AVN roadmaps that are designed to help implement AVNExcellence are based on researching the best practices of 100's of incredibly successful accountants from around the UK, identifying what each do best and then bringing those best practices into a single set of standards that you can aspire toward achieving with the training, support and guidance of AVN.

90 If You Want To Be Interesting – Be Interested

It is a simple fact that most people are better talkers than listeners. There is the old expression that God gave us one mouth and two ears and perhaps we should use them in the same proportions.

If we really want to have a great relationship with our clients, we need to listen to them more. We need to be interested. As a result, we become interesting people and they will like and value us more because of it. Have great questions. Ask one and then sit back and listen to the answer and do not be afraid of a silence! Remember, different questions result in different conversations and different conversations result in different outcomes.

91 Do Not Always Concentrate On What Is Going Wrong But What Is Going Right

This is perhaps an alternative way of looking at things. When you think about it, most businesses and accountants are running a business, concentrate on what is not working in an effort to make it work. It seems sensible and possibly is, a lot of the time. However, perhaps we need to spend more time focusing on what is working rather than always on what is not!

If we look at what is going right in our business, will it perhaps tell us what we could do more of and how we might learn lessons in those areas that we might replicate in other parts of the business? I am not suggesting that we focus all our time in these areas, but perhaps some time. Certainly more than we currently do!

The very best thing about learning new stuff and applying it in your accountancy business is that you can replicate it with your clients and their businesses. It is even better and easier to talk to them about it because you can, with hand on heart, tell them what you have done and the **benefits** you gained from it. You are not talking theory, you are talking practice and that means you have real credibility with them, they believe and trust you more. They are more likely to say, "So how much will that cost me?" giving you a great opportunity to provide an additional service. The sad thing is that many accountants seem to detach their thinking from their own business and want to try and sell a new skill/knowledge they have obtained before thinking about how it can be applied in their own business. Do it on yourself and measure the benefits and then talk to your clients about what you have done and the **benefits** you gained from doing it.

92 Be Proactive

Nearly every accountant will tell you, either in conversation or on their website or other marketing material, that they are proactive. Sadly, this is rarely true!

Simply ask yourself a simple question. How many times in the last month...
- Did I contact a client without being asked...
- ...and make a suggestion to that client which was timely, relevant and free of any costs?

If you can honestly say that you have done that sometimes, then ask yourself:
- Have I done that in the last month for all of my best (grade A 1) clients? If you cannot say **yes** to that, you cannot truly claim to be proactive.

You need to systemise this process because it will not happen if you simply leave it to chance. And it is no good to say you are too busy. Ask yourself why am I too busy? Chances are you will find you are too busy doing the wrong things, chasing after the wrong clients. And those will be clients who give you 80% of the grief and provide you with 20% of the revenue and probably no profit at all. They are stopping you from being proactive and working with your most valuable clients. Those are the clients who provide you with nearly all of your profit.

93 Always Have An Open Mind

Well more of an open one anyway!

Never say "That won't work for us" or "The trouble is, we have a different kind of client." It is amazing how many accountants think like this. I believe we become totally blinkered in the way we see things and are rarely prepared to accept new ideas or ways of doing things. So many accountants have told me that it 'May work for someone else, but it won't work here' or I get the 'We tried that, but it did not work'. When you ask them how many times and you push hard, they usually say "We tried it once!" Just because it did not work the first time does not mean it will not work at all. If it works for others it simply means that we are not trying hard enough or are not persistent enough or are not quite doing the right things or perhaps in the right order.

Being critical of new ideas is fine, but we should always maintain the balance between having an open and a closed mind.

94 Encourage Complaints!

I remember asking one of my partners to ask his clients "How do you think we have done?" He looked at me a bit horrified and said, "I can't do that. What if they say we have not done very well!"

The answer is of course, we want to know before anybody else does. If you know you have fouled things up and you get to know about it, you have a chance to put things right. If you put things right very quickly you have a great chance of impressing your client and turning a difficult situation into a very promising one.

You will recall in number 26 that I referred to the story about a garden machinery company. Well that example works brilliantly here as well. They used to send out faulty machines to customers quite deliberately! Not dangerous faulty machines of course, but something that that the customers needed to contact them about to correct. When that happened, they reacted very quickly and impressed the customer with the manner in which they rectified the fault. The customer was of course, very happy and it created a great relationship with the customer going forward. The customer would no doubt be initially very displeased but would then be impressed, forgetting the initial problem and would then tell others how good the company was at rectifying the fault. Whether this is totally true, I am not sure but you can understand the logic in getting customers to be honest about your service so that you can improve and impress!

HOW AVN CAN HELP
There is a great training resource called 'How to never lose another customer' in System Builder. It goes through how to deal with customer issues in the best possible way so that even after you've made a mistake they still think you're great.

95 Perception Is Reality

I never really thought much about the word 'perception'. It never really occurred to me that it was a very important word.

I remember going to my AVN MasterClass in Leeds in May 1999 and Steve Pipe talked about 'perception being reality'. At least it is for the person who perceives it! What they think is real to them is real.

Most of us see things in a way we understand. It is as it is! For us it is anyway. However, someone else they may see it differently. When trying to explain to someone else it is very frustrating when they don't get it. Why do they not see what we see? They perceive something else and it is real for them. We need to understand what it is they see and then endeavour to explain what it is that we see.

Stephen Covey, in his book – '7 Habits' which I referred to earlier, asks us to seek to understand before being understood. Quite simply, if we can understand what they are seeing then we are far better able to explain our own position and what we see! But remember, because someone sees it differently to you does not mean they are wrong. Understand where they are and you will be better able to explain what you see.

96 Simple But True

There are many people who have taught me many things over the years, particularly over the last 15 or so. These people have many sayings and expressions which I love because they are so true, full of common sense and very memorable.

Some of these are:

- What is the definition of madness – to carry on doing the same things and expect to get a different result!
  And the message is – be brave and do something new.
- When was the best time to plant a tree? Answer, probably around twenty years ago. When is the next best time? Today.
  And the message is – do not prevaricate. Get on and do things because it is never too late.
- Is what I do today going to take me closer to my goal?
  If it is not going to, why am I doing it?
  And the message is – only do what takes you closer to achieving what you want. Do not waste your time doing other stuff.
- More people talk about a bad experience than talk about a good one!
  And the message is – if something goes wrong, put it right as quickly as you can. Suddenly you have got something positive rather than a negative.
- Nobody talks about an average experience, only a good or a bad one.
  And the message is – never be just average and you do not want to be bad! Be brilliant!
- Seek to understand before being understood (Stephen Covey's book – 'The 7 Habits of Highly Effective People').
  And the message is – Learn to listen and understand people's point of view before explaining yours! You are more likely to have a positive result.

HOW AVN CAN HELP

My personal expression which I'll add to the pot is 'When would now be a good time?' You've almost reached the end of this book now, what are you going to do with what you've learned? What action will you take? When will you take it? Download the AVN Action Planner and begin assigning actions to yourself and involve others in your team. Remember that your Practice Growth Expert is at the end of the phone or perhaps you're due to attend a peer group session. If there's anything from this book or my points that you require further discussion about, talk to AVN.

97 Use These Ideas With Your Customers

If you think any of these ideas are useful in your business, imagine how useful they may be in your customers' businesses. There is no better way of making a recommendation to a customer than by saying, "We did this for ourselves and the benefits for us were..." Then you tell them what they were. How can you, with any credibility, suggest something to your customer that you have not tried for yourselves? And yet so many of us do. The first thing they will ask you is, "Have you done this?" It's hardly a recommendation to then say, "Well, we are thinking about it, but have not done it yet..."

I am not suggesting that all the ideas in this short book will work for all your customers, but some will and of course they will be different for different customers. Be selective and be brave!

HOW AVN CAN HELP
Remember that your Practice Growth Expert is at the end of the phone or perhaps you're due to attend a peer group session. If there's anything from this book or my points that you require further discussion about, talk to AVN.

Conclusion

As I said at the very beginning, this book is not an academic book and it was never intended to be. It started out as a way of simply capturing some of the things I have learnt from a number of people, mostly over the period from 1997 to date. The order of the ideas is a bit haphazard and that is mainly because there is a thread through most if it, although not all.

Most of what I have written is common sense. Nothing clever at all! The only clever bit is that much common sense is not commonly used. So, if you practice it, perhaps you will be cleverer than some others.

I hope some of the ideas make you think. I hope most will be helpful to you, but remember they only work if you take action to make them work. That is the biggest mistake many of us make. We think about something, but we do nothing.

Be brave, take action and make things happen!

About the Author

Jonathan Holroyd was born in 1947 and is married with a son and daughter. He qualified as a Chartered Accountant in 1972 and set up as a sole practitioner in York in 1976. He acquired a small practice in Filey in 1982 and merged with a multi-partner practice in York in 1986; this practice becoming Hunter Gee Holroyd (HGH).
He subsequently became senior partner in 1997.

Having learnt of AVN, he led his firm to become founding members. On his retirement he joined the team at AVN and then went on to mentor over 100 member firms. He continues to work with a small number of these businesses.

Jonathan was also responsible for the development of the AVN software, GoalGetter. The inspiration for this came from all he learnt with AVN and Durham Busiess School where he studied in the last year at HGH.

Notes

Notes

Notes

Notes